Eamon Evans is a Melbourne-based writer who has spent all his working life writing for the online and print media. His work has appeared in *The Sunday Herald Sun*, *The Adelaide Advertiser*, *Australian Book Review*, *The Sunday Times* and *The Courier-Mail.* Online, he has been an in-house writer for *BigPond Sport*, *SBS*, *ArtsHub*, the *Weekly Book Newsletter* and the electronic bulletin of the International Federation of Arts Councils and Culture Agencies. Eamon Evans is the author of 15 books, one or two of them pretty good. He lives in Melbourne.

THE LUCKY COUNTRY

EAMON EVANS

First published by Affirm Press in 2023
Boon Wurrung Country
28 Thistlethwaite Street
South Melbourne VIC 3205
affirmpress.com.au

10 9 8 7 6 5 4 3 2 1

A catalogue record for this book is available from the National Library of Australia

ISBN: 9781922848437 (paperback)

Cover design by Josh Durham/Design by Committee © Affirm Press
Typeset in Garamond Premier Pro by J&M Typesetting
Proudly printed in Australia by McPherson's Printing Group

To Merran Evans, whose idea this was and who I'm lucky to have as a mum

Contents

Introduction

One sunny morning back in 1963, a young Sydney journalist picked up a pen, closed the door of his study, and sat himself down at his desk.

Like many a writer before him, Donald Horne had promised his publisher a masterpiece. A manuscript that might sway the fate of nations. A book that could help change the world. With its penetrating insights and crisp, biting prose, *Anatomy of Australia* was not just going to take on Australia's ruling elite. It was going to take them right down.

Before that, though, I'm betting that Donald discovered a need to clean up his desk, and then find a few extra pens. That creak in the door may have also needed addressing, right away, which would have required a quick trip to the store. And since he was down there already, it would have just made good sense to pick up some milk, post a letter, get petrol and attend to one or two minor chores. Procrastination is often associated with laziness, but it is actually a lot of hard work. I suspect that by the end of that first week, every square inch of Donald's house would have been swept free of dust and every one of his socks would have been folded in pairs.

But by the end of the year, Donald didn't just have an alphabetised bookshelf and a complicated new system for ironing his shirts. Unlike many writers before him, he had actually written himself a nice, shiny book.

And what a book! A searing indictment of Menzies Australia; a scathing critique of our smug, shallow culture. If any of its readers had ever wondered if they might have any faults, then Donald was here to put all doubts to rest. He was here to hold up a mirror to Australian society. And he didn't expect people to like what they saw.

Essentially a series of essays, Donald's basic thesis was that Australia was like a spoilt, lazy child. A child who has had the good luck to inherit a fortune from Mother England in the form of peace, wealth, art, democracy and the rule of law, but who has taken this inheritance for granted and never done much for themselves. A child who has never had to work. A child who has never had to fight. A child who has never had to think, learn or grow.

The result (in the early 60s, at least) was a 'nation without a mind': a nation of 'mediocre' 'philistines' who 'show less enterprise than almost any other prosperous industrial society'. Or, to quote the famous late-addition line that gave *Anatomy of Australia* its last-minute name change: 'a lucky country run mainly by second-rate people who share its luck ... and live on other people's ideas'.

'A bucket of cold salt water emptied onto the belly of a dreaming sunbather,' *The Lucky Country* was surprisingly well-received by the public. (Much like that time I won an argument with my partner.

Though she did change her mind back again the next day.) Nothing less than a commercial sensation, it sold out completely in under a fortnight and remained a bestseller for more than four years. A 'classic of pop-sociology', it is still remembered and quoted today.

Might this not rather suggest that Donald was wrong? That he was actually living in a nation of self-critical intellectuals? A nation dedicated to self-analysis and growth?

No. It suggests that he had a good title. The thing about classic books, as we all know, is that most people don't really read them. But a good title can really catch on. Think 'Jekyll and Hyde', 'time machine', 'catch 22', 'Sophie's choice'. All well-known phrases that are used all the time ... by people who have not read the books. Which is perfectly acceptable, provided you remember one thing: you can't judge a book by its cover. Mice don't turn up in *Of Mice and Men* and that whole 'catcher in the rye' thing is some kind of metaphor. Actual rye grass is not involved in any way, just as there are no actual mockingbirds in *To Kill a Mockingbird* or fruit in *A Clockwork Orange*.

By the same logic, there was nothing in Horne's title that was supposed to be positive. It was supposed to be darkly ironic. It was intended as a term of reproach.

Instead, here we are. In a land we all call 'the lucky country'. A phrase that, somewhere along the line, we apparently just decided to completely accept at face value and embrace as a cute badge of pride. 'I have had to sit through the most appalling rubbish as successive generations misapplied this phrase,' Donald complained decades later, about the nickname that became his chief legacy. Instead of a brutal wake-up call, his book had accidentally ended up giving Australians a brand-new reason to feel slightly smug. A brand-new way to essentially say 'no worries'. A brand-new reason to think 'she'll be right'.

But here's the thing, folks. Maybe ... just maybe ... she *will* actually be right. Maybe our nation's nickname isn't rubbish at all. Maybe we really are lucky?

Why? Well, for starters, just take a look at the place. It's beautiful. It's warm. It's got fresh air and clean water. And it's far away from the world's warzones.

Better still: it's absolutely massive. We're talking 7.69 million square kilometres. That's about 5 per cent of the world's total land area. And 5 per cent that's home to only about 0.3 per cent of the world's total people. England, for purpose of illustration, has about 434 citizens per square kilometre, while China has about 149. Down here in the lucky country, we have around about three. That is a lot of elbow room. That's a lot of big houses and a lot of big yards. And a lot of big parks and a lot of big pools and a lot of big beaches and forests. Plus footy ovals. And tennis courts. And golf courses. And bike tracks. And places to bowl or play basketball. Australia is incredibly fortunate to be a nation of wide, open spaces. A nation of clean, green places where people can jog and ride and swim. Or, if they prefer, put a shrimp on the barbie.

We've also got plenty of places for people to build, dig and farm. Australians all let us rejoice, for we truly are the lucky country when it comes to the fruits of land. We have copper and gold and meat and wheat; we have wool, iron and coal. There's golden soil and wealth for toil and our home is girt by sea. Our land abounds in nature's gifts and we are young and free.

But however lucky we may be to have these resources, we are also lucky to live in a place that's (more or less) very well run. Whatever Australia's economic failures may have been in the 60s (and however much the mineral boom may have helped us out since), I think it's fair to say that Donald's spoilt child has been growing up pretty fast. It's been thirty full years since our last real recession: thirty years of smooth, steady growth. No other OECD country has been able to achieve this. In fact, they haven't even come close. The Australia of today is essentially far more prosperous and successful than any of the many nations that Horne felt were outdoing us.

I would also say that Australia has become a well-*rounded* adult, not just a well-off one. Exhibit one: our wealth is (fairly!) evenly distributed. We're pretty egalitarian, compared to most countries. Whether or not they can afford to eat smashed avocados or pay off their mortgage within the next 100 years, the 'average Australian' is actually better off than the average citizen of any other country, according to data from Credit Suisse. And if you're below average, we at least have a welfare system that's not a complete joke (though some would say that it's well on the way).

And Australians aren't just very wealthy, we're also very healthy, with the world's fourth-highest level of life expectancy. That's thanks to a healthcare system that's not only free but – in world terms – absolutely first class. Our public schools are good (and probably won't get you shot), while our universities are not only affordable, but attract students from all over the world.

I could go on and on. So I guess I may as well. For all the sensationalist headlines you sometimes see in the tabloids, Australian society is extremely harmonious. Our neighbourhoods are safe, our crime rates are low, our different communities are all pretty cohesive. You're much more likely to see people from different ethnicities laughing and chatting and having a drink, than exchanging words or getting into a brawl.

Racism, of course, remains a real issue – but it's hard to think of a place where it doesn't. And it's easy to think of places that clearly have it much worse. For all the work that's still to be done, I think it's safe to call Australian multiculturalism a monumental success story. At least half of us are migrants or the children of migrants but we function as one sweet whole. A single, proud and tolerant nation. United in our contempt for New Zealand.

And all that's just for starters. We're also lucky to have stable government; great wine and beer; excellent cafes; first-class restaurants; fresh fruit and vegies; superb meat and seafood; good theatres and bookshops; beautiful animals; the Great Barrier Reef and God knows how many beaches. Throw in rubbish-free footpaths, pot-hole-free roads and the fact that George Pell is now dead, and it's really not any wonder that both the Economist Intelligence Unit and the UN's Human Development Index say that we're one of the world's best places to live. In short, we really are the lucky country. The Australia Donald described has long since evolved but there's a good reason why we still have the nickname. Australia has real problems, which really do need addressing, and I'm not just talking about that last album from Shannon Noll. But they're not really problems that you'd think about in most developing countries. Or, for that matter, most countries, full stop.

Living in Australia is like winning the lottery. Or, if not a lottery, then at least a chook raffle or some office sweep. Set aside stuff like the Logies, and men who wear lycra, and we are actually all very lucky to live here, even if it doesn't feel like that all of the time.

And quite a few of us are luckier still. As the rest of this book will establish with Economic Intelligence Unit style rigour, Australia is not just home to a world-class standard of living. It's also home to some world-class flukes. Call them strokes of luck. Call them acts of God. Call them windfalls or twists of fate.

Personally, I call them useful material for the book that I promised my publishers an embarrassingly long time ago. Material that I'm going to start writing about right about now. Just as soon as I clean up this desk.

PART ONE

HAPPY ACCIDENTS

All religions have at least one thing in common, and I don't just mean the fact that they're wrong. I'm referring to the fact that, at bottom, they all share one belief: the belief that *stuff happens for a reason*. That somewhere out there is some kind of system or logic or (however loose) set of laws that helps to explain how life works. That when something bad happens, and you wonder 'why me?', somewhere out there, there will be some kind of answer. Because [insert name of deity] has some kind of plan.

Some call this plan divine will. Some call it destiny or fate. Some call it Tao, karma or yin and yang.

Personally, however, I call it horseshit. As a fully grown man who's never quite managed to do maths, or assemble IKEA furniture without my mum's help, it feels wrong to just casually dismiss so many complex belief systems – to just childishly shrug off so many generations of wisdom from so many people so much brighter than me.

But you've really, really got to trust me here, reader. They're all talking out of their arse. There is no plan. There is no system. Everything is randomness, chaos and chance. Life is like a poorly designed pinball machine with wobbly legs on a spinning ball prone to earthquakes and fire. When something bad happens and you wonder 'why me?', there is *not* actually an answer out there in the universe. Unless you count 'why the hell not?'

Here's the thing, though. Good things can happen too. Not because of God or dravya or Tao or Zeus or some crap you just read in your horoscope. Good things just happen because of good luck.

And it turns out that they happen a lot.

Born Lucky

Ever felt like you're not all that special?
Here's exactly why you are wrong

'You are lucky to be alive. Inhale and take in life's wonders. Never take so much as a single petal of a flower for granted.'

Matt Haig, UK author and journalist

Shall we start this book on a positive note? With some glad tidings designed to bring forth good cheer?

Well, why not? There's enough grim stuff in the world these days, what with climate change and COVID and famine and war and that little bald patch on the back of my head.

So here it is (the good news, not the bald patch): you can forget all about social convention. Presuming that you've hit the age of eighteen, there's absolutely no one to stop you doing just what you want, provided it does not affect others. You can sleep through the day.

You can drink half the night. You can shun social contact and only eat chips. Want to drink too much? Wear old trakky daks? Never clean the house or get up from your couch? Well, the good news is that you can feel free to do so. By all means, just go right ahead. Close your eyes and carpe that diem. Sit down and seize the day.

The bad news, however, is that you sound like you might be depressed. And if this is so, you are far from alone. Just like its cousins sadness and anxiety, depression is a serious and growing concern all throughout modern society. According to the National Study of Mental Health and Wellbeing 2020–21, over 43 per cent of adult Australians have experienced a mental disorder of some sort at some point in their lives. And I think that it's probably safe to say that the rest have all had low moments (especially if they've spent time in Geelong).

Life, all of this is to say, can sometimes feel pretty hard. We all know what it's like to feel a little bit shit – to feel like someone else is somehow doing life 'better'. Maybe they're more popular? Maybe they're more successful? Maybe they have a nice house and show no signs of balding?

Well ... maybe they do. As this book will tell you, time and time again, some people really do catch some great breaks. Some people really are just born lucky.

But here's a thought to keep in mind the next time you feel a bit down. We are *all* born lucky. You, me, that dickhead next door. The woman at your work with weird glasses.

Reason being: we were born in the first place. Forget about how you're 'going' in life and just reflect, for a time, on the *fact* of it. The fact that you exist – that you can breathe, think and fart – is not an incidental little thing that you should just take for granted. It is a mind-boggling fluke. A stupendous piece of luck. A freakishly unlikely stroke of good fortune.

Don't believe me? You sound like my kids. But perhaps you'll believe Dr Ali Binazir. Educated at Harvard and Cambridge, and not afraid of a ridiculous number, that academic once set out to calculate the odds of any given person being born (be they you, me or weird-glasses-lady). The answer, he eventually concluded, is one in $10^{2,685,000}$. Yes, that's the number 10 to the power of 2,685,000.

Spelled out in full, that's a very, very big number – in fact, a number far, far too big to fit in this book. A number too big, in fact, to fit in an entire library full of books. Or in every single book that has ever been printed. Ridiculous numbers like this can be hard to get our heads around, so Dr Binazir provides this analogy, which just uses huge ones. The probability of you being born, he suggests, is equivalent to the probability of rolling a trillion-sided dice two million times ... and coming up with exactly the same number on every single occasion.

The bottom line, dear reader, is that you are a miracle. And in even more happy news, so am I. A walking, talking, sweating, balding miracle, who may be a bit overweight these days but is soon going to cut out carbs. There will always be times (like when we hop on some scales) when we miracles can't help but feel bad. But the fact that we can feel *anything whatsoever* is absolutely extraordinary. And, as such, an extraordinary privilege.

So *why* is being born so wildly improbable?

Well, for starters, just look up.

To understate things just a touch, there's a lot of stuff to see up there. The universe is eye-poppingly vast. Even if you were to travel at light speed (that's 300,000 kilometres per second), you wouldn't be able to get from one end to the other in a couple of days or a couple of weeks. Or a couple of months, years or decades. You'd need about 93 billion years. (Or even more if you stop for a pee.)

During these billions of years, you'd see something like a trillion galaxies, every single one of them filled with billions of planets.

But there's every reason to doubt that you'd see conscious life.

No one can really know, of course, but plenty of highly decorated astronomers are pretty sure that we on Earth are alone. This planet may have its problems (e.g. people who eat Chiko Rolls) but, as astrobiologist David Waltham says, it's also 'a precious jewel'. You and I may well be living in an intergalactic one-off – a unique rock that's been blessed with 'a rare combination of qualities that happen to make it almost perfect for life'.

And even said rock only arrived pretty recently. It's worth remembering that for the first two-thirds of the universe's 13-billion-year history, this precious jewel didn't even exist. It wasn't until about 8.5 billion long years after the Big Bang ago that gas, dust and asteroids slowly began to merge into the planet we call home – and even then, it was too hot to live in. Boiling enough to fry an egg, and then melt the entire pan, Earth was your usual barren, noxious, uninhabitable wasteland. Think Venus and Mercury and Saturn and so on: radioactive rocks, poisonous gases and weird gravitational stuff that would snap you in half.

And it's also worth remembering that Earth's current 'preciousness' won't last for long. In about six billion years, the sun will start to get a lot bigger, and a hell of a lot hotter, and eventually wipe out all life as we know it.

But in the meantime, here we are. In a uniquely habitable place at a uniquely habitable time. So, what had to happen to make all this possible?

The very, very (very) short answer is that Earth had five strokes of luck – the first being its ideal location. Right at this moment, the Earth just happens to be the perfect distance from a perfectly sized star (a star which we, of course, call the sun). Astronomers call this highly exclusive slice of real estate 'the Goldilocks zone': not too hot and not too cold, and 'just right' when it comes to gravitational stability.

Stroke of luck number two is that Earth somehow has water – and, just as remarkably, somehow managed to keep it. Why didn't all that H_2O evaporate during Earth's first billion or so years, when the whole place was piping hot? Probably because at least a little bit was buried deep underground.

But these first two strokes of luck may not be all *that* uncommon. Mars, for example, may have once had liquid water before it all turned to steam, and astronomers have identified quite a few faraway planets that also seem to be in a Goldilocks zone. Kepler-1649c and Gliese 3293d *could* both be chock-full of aliens.

The point, though, is that's absolutely no reason why they *should* be. Yes, 'Earth-like' conditions are needed to sustain life, whatever form it might come in. But they do not in any way serve to *create* it. How life actually *began* remains a major mystery. Today's biologists have invented all sorts of stuff, from cancer-fighting immune cells to Dolly the sheep, but they could not even *begin* to create cells from scratch. The starting point of a new cell is always some other cell. Everything we can do in the field of biology requires the prior existence of biology itself.

Which brings us to stroke of luck number three: the fact that planet Earth somehow knew what to do once things had cooled down a touch. About 3.7 billion years ago, on some random day in some random pond, something truly miraculous seems to have occurred. Out of *literally* nowhere – and I mean 'literally' very literally – some kind of single-celled organism appeared out of the blue. A single-celled organism that somehow found a way to reproduce itself and ever-so-slowly evolve.

But when I say 'ever-so-slowly,' I really do mean it. For the next three billion years or so, bacteria and algae and other such microbes were about as sophisticated as life on Earth got. If our planet's history was compressed into twenty-four hours – i.e. if Earth came into being at the first stroke of midnight – you would have needed a waterproof microscope to see any sign of life before about 10pm. (And chances are that, if there is indeed life on another planet, this is the sort of thing it would be. Forget little green men with spaceships and lasers. If aliens actually live on Kepler-1649c, they are probably some kind of green fungus.)

So what exactly happened at 10pm? How did Earth make that journey from miniscule pond scum to multi-celled organisms – to a planet filled with plants, animals and people (along with lower life forms like Peter Dutton)? The answer lies with stroke of luck number four: the fact that, somewhere or other, some group of enterprising microbes somehow started to develop 'a miraculous skill'. This was photosynthesis. The ability to suck up water and sunlight and somehow turn it all into oxygen.

But all that lovely oxygen would have just gone to waste were it not for the biggest miracle of all – AKA stroke of luck number five. I'm talking about the random day in some random pond when two random cells suddenly decided to merge. We don't know why. We don't know how. But we do know that these two single-cell organisms instantly became a *two*-celled organism. A two-celled organism with a 'eukaryotic' structure, which allowed it to keep on merging elsewhere. Every animal and plant today shares that eukaryotic cell structure. Every plant and animal today is that two-celled organism's direct descendant.

Biologists call this merger the 'Fateful Encounter' and are 'very confident that it only happened once'. As *New Scientist* explains, 'if simple cells had slowly evolved into more complex ones over billions of years, all kinds of intermediate cells would have existed, and some still should. But there are none.' In other words, if mergers between single-cell organisms were reasonably common, the Earth would be full of organisms with only two cells (and probably lots with just a small handful).

But it isn't. On Earth, living things either have just one single cell (like, say, meningococcus) or what you might call a shitload. Even a tiny little fly has about five million of the things, while your average ant has around twenty million.

This rather suggests that 'simple cells just don't have the right cellular architecture to evolve into more complex forms'. Which in turn suggest that there was nothing 'natural' or inevitable about the Fateful Encounter. It was a 'freak accident'. A 'shockingly rare anomaly'. A chance event that has occurred only once and is thus unlikely to occur ever again. The existence of complex life is a miracle, in other words. An event so unlikely as to be almost impossible.

But the true miracle, of course, is the existence of complex *you*. The complex organism that is currently reading this book, and thinking that, in some way, they are a little bit crap.

Please vanquish that thought. Please kill it with fire. Please flush it down the toilet and then press flush again.

Because you, my friend, are an absolute freaking miracle. And I'm not saying that because you still like to read books.

I'm saying it because of all your unborn siblings – because all of those hundreds of millions of speedy spermatozoa that you somehow managed to beat in that race to the egg. You were the winner, so congratulations to you, and please enjoy the reward that is life.

But even that lucky break is only half of the story. To get the exact DNA sequence that has made you *you*, and not some opera-loving bus driver, acne-riddled baker or beady-eyed accountant who likes to play Lego, that little sperm of your dad's didn't just have to come first (so to speak). It had to come first in just the right race. A race with just the right egg at the finish line.

Mathematically speaking, this is no mean feat, given the average future mum tends to have about 300,000 eggs. The average male, for his part, will produce something like 525 billion sperm over the course of his life (or even more if he has access to the internet).

So the chances of the particular sperm that provided half your DNA getting together with the particular egg that provided the other half were not just small. They were impossibly, vanishingly, laughably small, even if your parents had had sex twenty-five times a day, for twenty-five years, in between courses of IVF.

Sorry. Yucky image. I'm sure that they didn't do that. In fact, when you stop and think about it for a moment, it's actually pretty extraordinary that they had sex at all.

For all that your mum and dad may seem like regular people there's a very real sense in which they are total one-offs. Just like you and me and Van Gogh and Napoleon, they are each made up of 37 trillion or so entirely unique little cells. Each one containing a DNA code that is unlike anything anywhere in the world.

For you to exist, these two one-offs in the history of the universe did not just need to have sex in precisely the right way, and on precisely the right day, and let Dame Luck do all the rest. They both had to be alive at the same point in history. They both had to somehow cross paths. They both had to be healthy, horny and at least vaguely attractive, and then choose to shag at least once. Or, more likely, to form a relationship for as long as it took to shag that one single time when your sperm and egg merged.

Now, I don't know about you, but in my case meeting people doesn't always lead to my shagging them – even back in the days when I had a full head of hair. And according to less-than-scientific studies of the sort that are endlessly cited online, in this I am very far from alone. Apparently, the average person tends to meet about 80,000 people in the course of their life – i.e. about 0.001 per cent of the planet. Of those, each person rarely sleeps with more than about twenty-four others – that's a strike rate of 0.00000003 per cent. So be sure to thank your mum and dad the next time you see them, for being so kind as to get down to business (or, if you prefer, have a bone, bang or bonk).

But, while you're on the topic, you should probably be thanking your grandparents for being fuck buddies too. Because for your mum to be your mum, and your dad to be your dad – for these two utterly unique genetic entities to exist in the first place, and so make the utterly unique genetic entity that is you – their mums and dads needed to be *their* mums and dads. The precise sexual encounters that created each of your parents are just as far-fetched, improbable and frankly fantastical as the precise sexual encounter that created you. But they needed to happen first, for your birth to take place.

And the story of you certainly doesn't stop there. Because we're not just talking about a preposterously unlikely sexual encounter between two parents. And we're not just talking about the four grandparents that, er, came before them. We're talking about preposterously unlikely shags between eight great-grandparents, sixteen great-great-grandparents, thirty-two great-great-great-grandparents and sixty-four great-great-great-great-grandparents.

And even then, the story's just getting started. Do you think 16,384 great-great-great-great-great-great-great-great-great-great grandparents sounds like a big number? Well, that only takes us back about 350 years – to a time of heaving bosoms and extra-tight tights, rakes, bucks and coy, winsome maids. If even a single one of those 16,384 ancestors had not shagged precisely the right person at precisely the right time, you, reader, would just not exist.

The story of your genetic good fortune stretches way back beyond that – back to long before the time people did their wooing in caves. In fact, it goes all the way back to that Fateful Encounter. You are just the latest in an unbroken string of statistical anomalies that could and should have been snapped any time.

So, the next time that life starts to get you down – the next time you get fired; the next time you get dumped; the next time you don't cut the mustard – I would suggest that you reach for a mirror. Try not to dwell on the bald spot. Just stand back and admire what you see.

What you can see is a biological aristocrat: you are the distinguished heir of an unbroken lineage that goes back literally billions of years. The final links in a long, long chain of events, each one so far-fetched as to be almost impossible.

That means you are special. That means you're unique. That means you are a miracle.

To be born in the first place is to be born lucky. Life is a gift. So enjoy it.

Survival of the Luckiest

How an accident of geography helped humans not go extinct

'It's hard to detect good luck – it looks so much like something you've earned.'

Frank A Clark, US congressman

It was luck, more than anything, that led Charles Darwin to the round-the-world voyage that reshaped his career. Essentially a bit of an upper-class layabout who was all set to become a clergyman, this 'rather unmotivated' Cambridge graduate was not invited to become a ship's naturalist because he actually sought out the job, or had shown some great skill in the field. Studying animals was a hobby at most. His preference, in fact, was to hunt them.

So how did this thoroughly unremarkable twenty-two-year-old get to go to the Galápagos? The short answer is family connections. The *Beagle*'s equally well-born captain had no interest in spending five long years at sea with 'some damned collector of specimens'. If the voyage really *had* to bring some kind of swot aboard, then said swot would need to be a 'suitable companion': someone who knew how to dress for an eight-course dinner and discuss cricket over stilton and port. He 'would not take anyone, however good a Naturalist, who was not recommended to him likewise as a gentleman'.

This was good news for Darwin, who was certainly a gentleman. And over time he became a good naturalist too. Seeing similar-but-ever-so-slightly-different species scattered across different islands didn't just lead him to hunt them with hounds, while shouting 'pip-pip' and 'Tally ho!' It led him to wonder what drove all these differences. To wonder how and why different species evolve.

The answer, he famously decided, was 'natural selection'. This being the idea that an animal that is well-suited to its environment will generally live a little longer than one that is not. This generally means that they'll shag more too. Which generally means they pass on more of their genes.

The ancestors of giraffes, for example, had pretty normal-sized necks. Imagine a sort of weird-looking deer. Said 'deer' was perfectly well-suited to its environment, getting ample food from the lower branches of trees and whatever plants it could find on the ground. But then came a day the world's climate changed, and many of these plants were wiped out. With food so much scarcer, competition for it became stiffer. And the weird-looking deer that happened to have longer necks found themselves with a little slight. Being able to reach the higher parts of trees, they tended to survive a little longer than their short-necked relatives. And so they passed on their long-necked genes just a little bit more.

And that, in short, is natural selection. In the grim, ceaseless struggle for existence, the 'long necks' had an edge that allowed them to win. A competitive edge that quite literally grew over time, to the point where said necks are six feet long and their weird-looking ancestors are no longer with us.

And in that fate, they are far from alone. From the teeniest little mould spores to the hugest woolly mammoths, more than 99 per cent of all the species that ever roamed planet Earth nowadays roam it no more. The struggle for life has plenty of losers. It's not like a party game where every kid gets a prize. It's like a party game where most tend to get shot.

Darwin's theory is essentially a fact – but that's not quite how it was seen at the time. Even though Collingwood supporters have been around since 1892, it took a while for people to accept that we're apes, and not some divine creation specially favoured by God. We humans like to think that we're pretty special.

But eventually, we realised that we still could be. Because even if humans *are* only animals, it seems pretty clear that we are the best ones. Most species, after all, are well and truly extinct: history was a fight that they lost. We humans are still here, and clearly in charge. History was a fight that we won.

This is reasonable enough, as a statement of fact. But is it a reasonable basis for morality? In the 160 or so years since Darwin published his theory, many people have interpreted the process of 'natural selection' to mean something like 'might is right'. To mean that successful people must deserve their success, and society's 'failures' deserve only disdain. Basic social welfare measures, by this logic, ultimately just serve to preserve the stupid, and ensure that their genes get passed on. Forget public hospitals. Forget about the dole. If you don't cut the mustard, then you can suck eggs.

At its worst, the idea that life is a battle that the best always win has been used to justify everything from war on 'lesser' races, to laissez-faire capitalism, to the use of eugenics to wipe out disability. Fascists, colonisers, racists and businesspeople have done all sorts of dreadful things in the name of 'Social Darwinism', the most extreme example, of course, being Hitler. 'Earth,' that gentle soul proclaimed, is nothing more than 'a trophy cup for the industrious man. And this rightly so, in the service of natural selection. He who does not [win] does not deserve to possess the necessities of life.'

But such beliefs don't just lead us to be hard on each other. They can also mean that we're hard on ourselves. Didn't get that job? Didn't make the team? Didn't manage to not faint during that big speech for work, and then start to cry and/or fall off the stage? The reason was because, well, you clearly suck. People who fail essentially deserve to. That's just science. That is natural selection.

Well, I'm here to tell you to banish that thought. Put it in a pile with all your books by Dan Brown and then set the whole thing alight. Because that's not really 'science' at all.

Imagine that you were able to travel to an empty planet with water and sunlight and other Earth-like qualities, drop off a bunch of primitive organisms and then be on your way. Now imagine that your spaceship was also a time machine, which let you come back a few million years later. Do you think that you'd arrive on a planet with Earth-like inhabitants? A planet covered in mammals and birds and insects and fish, all under the thumb of a few hairless apes?

Well, think again. As Stephen Jay Gould wrote in *Wonderful Life*, 'Little quirks at the outset, occurring for no particular reason, unleash cascades of consequences that make a particular future seem inevitable in retrospect. But the slightest early nudge contacts a different groove, and history veers into another plausible channel, diverging continually from its original pathway.'

There was nothing inevitable about humans becoming nature's top dogs. Just as there was nothing inevitable about dinosaurs going extinct. Life is indeed a battle for survival, but who wins largely comes down to luck.

Look at dung beetles, for example. Or lemmings. Or sheep. Natural selection is not some historically inexorable, Nazi-style scheme designed to weed out the frail and the weak. It's a mindless response to the vagaries of chance: yes, species will often 'select' the best genes available, but whatever genes happen to be available to begin with simply come down to luck.

As biologist Paula Kover puts it in *The Conversation*, 'There are many organisms that are not perfectly adapted to their environment … Natural selection can only randomly favour the best of what is available, it does not purposefully turn all living organisms into one super creature.'

When you think about it, for example, we humans would be far better off if we could breathe underwater, instead of being stuck with these frail, land-bound bodies that can barely see, hear or smell. It's just bad luck that none of our ancestors happened to be blessed with a genetic mutation that worked like a gill. (Or maybe someone *did* but nobody shagged them. Because … well … we're talking about someone with gills.)

And even when an animal really is perfectly adapted to their environment, there's nothing to stop that environment from suddenly deciding to change. It's worth remembering that Australia used to be filled with gigantic wombats, and vicious echidnas that were the size of sheep. Like the sabre-toothed tiger and the T-rex before them, these 'super' animals were apex predators: state-of-the-art killing machines in perfect working order. And just like the sabre-toothed tiger and T-rex before them, these perfect apex predators are both now extinct.

Why are they gone, while the witchetty grub is still with us? Because their environment changed in a very abrupt, dramatic and – yes – unlucky way, which completely changed the rules of the game. And as science journalist Michael Greshko writes in *National Geographic*, the rate of extinction over the years has been very 'far from constant'. Most extinct species didn't slowly lose out in some long-term battle for survival; didn't slowly fade away due to some genetic flaw, which revealed itself over millions of years.

Instead, around 90 per cent of all the species that ever lived were wiped out during one of a small handful of huge ecological catastrophes. During what Greshko calls 'geological blinks of an eye'.

Dinosaurs, for example, were doing just fine in the battle for life, until some huge asteroid decided to crash into Earth and wipe out just about all their food. But what was bad luck for that species was good luck for ours, for it created the conditions for tiny mammals to flourish. Finally able to eat, sleep and shag without being attacked by some deranged giant lizard, these mammals slowly started to take over the planet and evolve into cats, dogs, cows, pigs and bears.

And then, about 300,000 years ago – the story goes – came the planet's true rulers: a newish species of primate from southern Africa. A primate that Swedes call *människor*, Germans call *menschen* and Italians refer to as *umani*. You and I, of course, call them humans.

Now if you look at deforestation and abattoirs and climate change and so forth, it could be argued that this species was bad luck for the planet – that every other animal would be better off if we didn't exist. But for my own sake, at least, I'm quite pleased that I do – and the same goes for most of my family.

But this good news should, once again, really just be seen as good luck. There was nothing inevitable about *Homo sapiens* not dying out;

nothing preordained by the dictates of Darwinism.

As Yuval Noah Harari says in his book *Sapiens*:

> There was nothing special about humans. Nobody, least of all humans themselves, had any inkling that their descendants would one day walk on the moon, split the atom, fathom the genetic code and write history books ... They were insignificant animals with no more impact on their environments than gorillas, fireflies or jellyfish.

How can we know this for certain? Because plenty of other 'humans' didn't actually make it. *Homo sapiens* is just one of several big-brained, small-jawed species of ape to clamber down from trees, get about on two legs, hunt, gather and build stuff with stones. We have at least eight – and possibly many, many more – older cousins, all of whom were doing well in the battle for survival long before *Homo sapiens* even got in the ring.

The first members of the genus Homo, *Homo habilis*, seem to have evolved out of some sort of African primate 2.5 million years ago. From there they travelled (on two legs) to all sorts of places, evolving in all sorts of ways. *Homo neanderthalensis*, for example, developed stocky thickset bodies that would have helped them to survive the cold climate in Europe. *Homo erectus*, on the other hand, seem to have been reasonably svelte, just like *Homo soloensis, Homo floresiensis* and the rest of their neighbours in the steamy south-east of Asia. What's now Russia was home to *Homo denisova*, while *Homo ergaster* and *Homo rudolfensis* seem to have stayed put in Africa, where they spent time avoiding *Homo heidelbergensis*.

So, when *Homo sapiens* turned up in southern Africa about 300,000 years ago, being a 'human' was far from unique. Just like there are many species of dogs – from Great Danes to Dachshunds and Chihuahuas – we were just the latest in a long and rather unremarkable line of cousins, most of whom were still around.

But now all of those are gone. They're kaputski. Extinct. And the culprit is almost certainly one or two ecological catastrophes – one or two cases of good old bad luck. The first seems to have been a 70,000-year-long cold spell that began 195,000 years ago and turned much of the planet into a kind of 'ice desert'. Then about 50,000 years after that, Earth's temperatures plummeted again, courtesy of a super volcano. The Toba eruption is thought to have led to a thousand-year volcanic winter, because so much ash and sulphur was blown into the air it largely blocked out the sun.

These were definitely not great times to be alive. But with edible plants and animals literally thin on the ground, they were definitely great times to die. And so (we think) that's exactly what our cousins did, in great and grim quantities all over the world.

But not *Homo sapiens*. They somehow survived. And in so doing, ensured that you're here.

How did they do this? Was it because they were smarter? Because they were better?

No. It was because they got lucky.

Thanks to DNA, we know that we humans have an *extraordinarily* low level of genetic diversity compared to most other animals. The most likely explanation for this is also the most simple one: at some very recent point in history, there were hardly any humans at all. That, just like 'three-quarters of planet life in the Northern Hemisphere', a whole lot of *Homo sapiens* were killed in two very short periods, and we all come from the tiny few who survived.

So what made these survivors so special? Nothing at all. What was special was the place where they lived. Humanity likely owes its existence to the fact that a small handful of *Homo sapiens* happened to live near the Cape of Good Hope. One of the few places on Earth to have been consistently inhabitable throughout the last 300,000 years, sit's home to what Scientific American calls 'the world's greatest diversity of geophytes' – geophytes being plants that largely grow and live underground. More or less impervious to cold, and very much able to grow all year round, geophytes are rich in complex carbohydrates, low in 'natural predators' and easy to dig up with a stick. In short, they're a perfect sort of 'survival kit' for 70,000 years of shit weather.

If that's not enough, the Cape is also home to a whole heap of shellfish. Full of proteins and omega-3 fatty acids, oysters, mussels and sea snails are all able to survive freezing temperatures. In fact, they're quite likely to thrive.

As archaeology professor Curtis Marean rather neatly conveys it, 'The small population that gave rise to all humans alive today may have survived by exploiting a unique combination of resources along the southern coast of Africa.'

It's to conveniently placed mussels and carbohydrate-rich corn that humanity owes its existence. Or, more to the point, it's to luck.

Remember that next time you fall off a stage, mid-speech. Then grit your teeth and clamber back up.

Serendipity

Accidental inventions and scientific discoveries

'The most exciting phrase to hear in science, the one that heralds new discoveries, is not "Eureka!" but, "That's funny."'

Isaac Asimov, US scientist and writer

Sri Lanka has had a few names in its time. It's been the Teardrop of India, the Granary of the East, Taprobana, Eelam and Ceylon. But for speakers of Persian, it was for a long time called 'Serendip'. And being a remote tropical island, filled with palm trees and peacocks, it is the perfect place to set the odd fairy tale.

Exhibit one: 'The Three Princes of Serendip', a tale first told in 1302. It features three princes who, for reasons too long and dull to go into, find themselves banished from their fabulous island kingdom and forced to wander throughout foreign lands. Over the course of their completely aimless (and extremely accident-prone) travels, they continually pick up random, seemingly trivial bits and pieces of information, which later prove to be hugely important. Thanks in part to the fact that the princes are smart, and able to connect dots that other characters miss, these little bits of trivia eventually add up to a few massive insights that help them to win wealth and fame.

Anyway, great story, if you like that kind of thing, but the key point here is that it produced a great word. I am of course talking about 'serendipity'. 'The faculty of making happy and unexpected discoveries by accident.'

But how useful is this word once we're in the real world? Is serendipity essentially a fairy tale? It's certainly true that most 'happy discoveries' can't really be called 'unexpected'. Most of the inventions that make our lives better tend to be slight tweaks on similar inventions that ever-so-slightly predated them, and that themselves built on things already made. Inventions are what you get when you take centuries of knowledge and put a few tedious boffins in a big, pricey lab. They're trial and error plus patience and repetition. Plus meetings and reports and budgets and committees and about eight million long, pointless emails. Basically, most inventions are what was probably always going to happen when a group of people decided to whittle away at a problem, day in and day out, for year after slightly dull year.

But other 'discoveries' were actually just what that sounds like. Unforeseen. Unlooked for. Unanticipated. Backarsewards. Sudden revelations and great big breakthroughs that more or less came out of nowhere. Crazy moments that simply would not have occurred were it not for a small slice of luck. After all, as William Beveridge once observed, 'It is scarcely possible to foresee a discovery that breaks really new ground, because it is often not in accord with current beliefs.'

Take the multi-channel cochlear implant, for example – AKA the bionic ear. The 1977 brainchild of Australia's own Graeme Clark, it represented arguably the biggest leap forward in hearing technology since the invention of the ear trumpet in 1634. Hearing aids, after all, are essentially just little microphones. All they can do is make a sound a bit louder. So they can only help people who can, to some degree, hear.

Bionic ears, on the other hand, can help almost anyone, even if a person can't hear at *all*. Reason being, they work in a different way. Clark's invention doesn't 'turn up' sounds, it turns them into something else – into a completely silent series of chemical and electronic impulses that somehow carry a sound *signal* all the way to your brain. If you think this sounds complicated, you would be correct. Said impulses must travel through a complex series of wires and interact with around 20,000 nerve fibres – a problem that, weirdly enough, paled in comparison to the challenge of getting all these wires to fit. Not only do they need to be small enough to squeeze inside a tiny cavity in your ear called the cochlea, they also have to weave their way along a spirally channel that's about a millimetre wide.

Even today, this sounds like sci-fi. Back in the early 70s, it just sounded ridiculous. But while Clark was an ear, nose and throat surgeon, he was also a man of great vision. Abandoning his lucrative surgical practice to pursue his vision, as a low-paid researcher at the University of Melbourne, the thirty-year-old spent years getting pretty much nowhere, all the while, according to the University of Sydney, 'meeting strong opposition from peers' and convinced he was wasting departmental money and time on a pointless pipe dream. 'There was even talk of forcing him to resign.'

Clark didn't give up, but he did go on holiday – taking his family to a beach in Minnamurra. A beach that just happened to be home to a shell that was shaped a lot like an ear. A shell that just happened to be lying next to a tuft of tall grass, precisely where Clark was sitting, while he watched his kids splash in the waves. A little bit bored by the entertainment on offer, as any parent will understand, he absent-mindedly grabbed a long and thin blade of grass and tried to thread it through the spiral-shaped channel in the shell.

'I realised that I could get a blade of grass to do what I needed the wires to do. The flexibility in the tip of the grass enabled it to negotiate around the turns of the shell.' Just like a blade of grass, his electrodes had to be more rigid at the base and more flexible at the tip. 'That was a flash of good fortune,' he said. Though a better word might have been 'serendipity'.

But while the bionic ear has helped thousands of people to hear, it's not really done much to help how they dress. An exacting fashion critic may well say that the same goes for velcro. But exacting fashion critics, as we all know, are by and large a bunch of almighty tools. When it comes to fastening fabrics together, velcro is the only name in the game.

The serendipitous invention of a Swiss engineer, velcro wasn't inspired by a walk on the beach – or some deep-rooted hatred of buttons and zips. It was inspired by a walk through the Alps and a deep-rooted interest in shooting small birds. During a summer holiday back in 1941, George de Mestral had had a lovely day outdoors, possibly yodelling a bit and eating fondue, in between maiming and killing everything he could see. But the day got a little less lovely once the thirty-three-year-old returned to his cabin and found that his pants were completely covered in cockleburs – sticky little seeds from an annoying local plant–which quickly proved a huge pain to remove.

There was nothing remotely new about this: cockleburs had been clinging to pants for centuries, and before pants to knickerbockers, breeches, robes, stockings and maybe even the odd Roman toga. But what was new was the fact that de Mestral wished to know why. Motivated by simple curiosity, rather than some desire to make tacky clothes, he took some cockleburs home, stuck them under a microscope and saw that each one contained hundreds of soft, tiny hooks. It took the future millionaire more than a decade to make a synthetic version of the hooks that were soft, flexible and not too sticky. But the basic idea for *vel*our *cro*chets ('velvet hooks') was born then and there. And it's a basic idea that probably would not exist if de Mestral had happened to go shooting elsewhere.

Another serendipitous invention that's stuck around, so to speak, is a product designed not to stick at all. Technically known as 'polytetrafluoroethylene', Teflon wasn't made to stop food from clinging to your frypan. It was made to help cool down your fridge.

This extraordinarily versatile material was the creation of one Roy J Plunkett, an Ohio chemist who worked with DuPont, back in the 1930s, when most fridges were cooled with sulphur dioxide. Curious to see if a cheap way could be found to prevent people from dying from a leak (or worse: getting ill and suing), he assembled a huge range of slightly less toxic chemicals to try to come up with an alternative coolant.

These chemicals included several canisters of a then-obscure gas, which Plunkett planned to play with somewhere down the track, but for which he had no immediate need. Not wanting it to 'go off', he duly arranged for it be frozen. But when the time finally came to unfreeze it, it was a gas no more. It had turned into a kind of white, waxy substance that was weirdly non-sticky. A white, waxy substance that now coats all your pans.

In the interests of brevity, I'm not going to list all the other everyday items that Teflon turns up in. (Though I suppose that the interests of brevity weren't really served by including a long pointless sentence to that effect. Or, I guess, by writing this sentence either. Let alone this one. Or this one. Or this.)

In the interests of a good Teflon segue, however, I feel honour-bound to mention that it's often used to make parkas – and that, for this serendipitous fact, we need to thank Robert Gore. Gore was a chemical engineer who just wanted to make a new kind of plumber's tape: a tape that could remain sticky even when it got wet. After a few years of getting more or less nowhere, Gore's thoughts turned to the frozen gas known as Teflon. Specifically: to what might happen if he heated it up. So he froze some polytetrafluoroethylene, stuck a few chunks in an oven, and then pulled one of them out with some tongs. Keen to see if it was still malleable enough to spread over sticky tape, his next step was to gently try to stretch a chunk out with his thickly gloved hands. But instead, it just snapped like a twig.

Undiscouraged, Gore tried it again with another hot chunk, this time even more slowly and lovingly, like a man trying to pat a sick kitten. Once again, it just snapped in two. And the same went for chunks three and four.

Sweaty and frustrated, Gore then snapped, giving the next chunk a sharp, angry tug. And wouldn't you know it, something weird happened. This one didn't snap, as he later recalled, but instead 'stretched the length of my arms. I was stunned.' By violently tugging the piping-hot polytetrafluoroethylene, Gore had accidentally 'uncoiled' its molecular structure, in a way that allowed it to soften and endlessly expand (and at the same time remain waterproof). He had accidentally created a product that you probably used the last time you tried on a parka, camped in a tent, or put on a hat, shoe or glove: Gore-Tex.

It's time for another segue, folks, and I'm afraid that what follows is the best that I've got. Parkas can be purple. So too shoes, tents and hats. Also worn by certain Wiggles, and fans of the Melbourne Storm, purple is a big, bold colour for people who like to make a big and bold statement (i.e. they need more attention or they don't have great taste).

But once upon a time, purple was a whole lot less common. In fact, it was the colour of royalty. A rare and special hue for rare and special people, it was a colour that Roman emperors could kill commoners for wearing, while Queen Elizabeth I preferred to issue a fine. The basic reason was that it was tricky and expensive to make. Good purple dye involved secreting a rare and hard-to-extract kind of mucus from a rare and hard-to-find kind of snail. Which, when you think about it, was also quite gross.

Nowadays, purple dye is quite common, in both senses of the word. It's easy to make, cheap to produce and, as such, no longer coveted. There's a moral about consumerism in that story somewhere, but let's skip to the part that involves serendipity. More specifically, it involves a teenage medical student called William Perkin, who was studying at London's Royal College of Physicians in 1856. The son of blue-collar workers, Perkin may not have been born with a silver spoon in his mouth, but he certainly had a heart of gold. So he was tickled pink when the college rolled out the red carpet and gave him the green light to use their laboratory to try to find a cure for malaria. He dutifully created a new medicine ... that did not cure malaria. But it was certainly a lovely rich purple.

Perkin is far from the only uni student to stuff up an assignment. Another one was Constantin Fahlberg. A chemistry student at Johns Hopkins University way back in 1879, Fahlberg spent much of his time analysing the chemical components of coal tar. Exactly what he was trying to achieve remains a bit of a head-scratcher, but the general idea seems to have been to advance human knowledge about a topic so boring that, until then, no one had bothered to study it.

And it seems fair to say that he had some success. Over to you, Constantin:

> One evening, I was so interested in my laboratory that I forgot about my supper till quite late, and then rushed off for a meal without stopping to wash my hands. I sat down, broke a piece of bread, and put it to my lips. It tasted unspeakably sweet. I did not ask why it was so, probably because I thought it was some cake or sweetmeat. I rinsed my mouth with water, and dried my moustache with my napkin, when, to my surprise the napkin tasted sweeter than the bread. Then I was puzzled. I again raised my goblet, and, as fortune would have it, applied my mouth where my fingers had touched it before. The water seemed like syrup. It flashed on me that I was the cause of the singular universal sweetness, and I accordingly tasted the end of my thumb, and found it surpassed any confectionery I had ever eaten. I saw the whole thing at once. I had discovered some coal tar substance which out-sugared sugar.

Constantin Fahlberg had, in fact, discovered anhydroorthosulphaminebenzoic acid. An artificial sweetener that needed a snappier name, and so nowadays is referred to as 'saccharine'.

Many decades later, US naval engineer Percy Spencer was hard at work during WWII, trying to find a better way to make magnetrons. A kind of 'high-powered vacuum tube oscillator', should those words happen to have any meaning, magnetrons were part of a top-secret radio detection and ranging (radar) system designed to help the Navy track enemy ships. But magnetrons also ended up being a part of most kitchens, because Spencer was a man who enjoyed a quick snack. A chocolate bar was tucked away in his pocket the day he was experimenting with a new type of magnetron tube. But he never got to eat the thing, because for some odd reason it had decided to melt.

Several experiments later, he managed to work out why – and give generations of bad, lazy cooks a way to get even worse. It turned out that magnetrons weren't just good at emitting radio waves. They were also great at emitting *heat*. This heat travels through microscopic electromagnetic waves – or 'microwaves,' as they are now better known.

Radio waves, while we're on the topic, also help to give us wi-fi – the technology that allows us to work from home (i.e. take naps and attend to small chores). But wi-fi itself would not really work in the first place, were it not for the fact that some CSIRO scientists had wanted to hear an exploding black hole.

This story really begins in the 1930s, when a US engineer named Karl Jansky was trying to radio a bunch of people all the way over in Europe and couldn't work out why the sound was so bad. He figured out that the answer didn't lie in the Atlantic, as he'd originally supposed, but from somewhere above our heads. It turned out that a lot of radio static is essentially the sound of the universe – i.e. the sound of other radio waves zooming about outer space. And colliding with one another. And interfering with each other. And just generally creating aural chaos.

This galactic cacophony is not a big problem for most radio listeners, who just want to tune into their local talkback or enjoy the sound of England losing at cricket. But for radio astronomers, it used to be a huge issue, because they were trying to hear stuff that was far, far away.

It wasn't until the 1970s that the Aussie scientists at CSIRO found a neat way to clean it all up, as part of their efforts to try and hear their black hole. They found a way to isolate and untangle the countless different cosmic waves and generally bring order to chaos. It was not an innovation that exactly made headlines at the time nor one that got anyone particularly excited. But it was a neat little solution to an extremely niche little problem (like telling your boss that you need to work 'offline' at home when you need a quick nap).

CSIRO never found its black hole, sadly. But it did find itself with an enormous head start when the World Wide Web was invented a few decades later, and clearly needed a way to be used without wires. Today, it holds several key wi-fi patents that bring in millions every year – all because someone reached for the stars.

Okay, that's enough serendipitous inventions for now. I need to go work offline.

The Luckiest Refugees

How an accident of geography shaped Australian history

'Luck is a very thin wire between survival and disaster, and not many people can keep their balance on it.'

Hunter S Thompson, US writer

For Australians, the Vietnam War finished in 1975. But for people who actually lived in the place, the bad times had only just begun. They now had to survive a repressive and violent communist regime (after years of having to put up with a corrupt, US-backed one).

So it's no surprise that the next ten years saw many of those folks try to flee. It's estimated that more than a million South Vietnamese mums, dad and kids crowded into cheap, leaky boats over the course of the decade to try their luck in the South China Sea. Many of them with no real knowledge of sailing. Many, many more in the face of huge storms. Factor in strong winds, wild currents, sharp rocks and Thai pirates, and it's even less of a surprise that around 300,000 'boat people' are thought to have perished in their quest for a less shitty life.

And on one pitch-black night back in 1981, that number looked set to grow. For it was on that night that ninety-nine 'weak and emaciated' would-be refugees found themselves adrift 500 kilometres out from shore, on a badly leaking boat built to hold sixty people. A boat whose two tiny engines had been broken beyond repair after four straight days of fierce, choppy storms. Most of the people aboard were dehydrated. Many had dysentery. And pretty much no one had food or water.

All were preparing to meet their maker. But they met the HMAS *Melbourne* instead. A gigantic Navy aircraft carrier that just happened to be passing by, after taking part in some international war games up north.

'I had never seen a big ship like that,' recalled the happy and healthy Australian citizen Stephen Nguyen, decades later, from his lovely home in the suburbs of Sydney. 'It was so huge ... and we had a very warm welcome by the sailors. We felt we were the luckiest refugees.'

'It was a miracle that they were discovered,' agrees the HMAS *Melbourne*'s Commander John Ingram. 'A number of them were at the point of unconsciousness [and] would have begun to die within hours, probably by dawn the next morning ... The sea is a very lonely place.'

The point of this story – which, I'm pleased to report, resulted in ninety-nine new Aussie citizens – is that the land down under is a hard place to get to. It's a long way away from anywhere, and (yes) girt by sea. Travelling to this country represents an extraordinarily long and dangerous undertaking for anyone not in a big, modern ship – or, better still, a big, modern plane.

So, the question becomes: how on earth did anyone manage it in the first place? How exactly did the first *Homo sapiens* actually get here from Africa 60,000 (or some such) years ago? We are talking, after all, about a journey of at least 10,000 kilometres. As the University of Queensland's Dr Michael Westaway has put it, in the context of the technology available back then, it was 'the equivalent of sending a spaceship to the moon'. And not only was there 'nothing comparable in human evolution at that time', there was no journey to compare to it afterwards, for many, many thousands of years.

Look at Ireland, for example. Or New Zealand. Or Greenland. Or Tonga. All those countries are islands, like us. They're all places that you can't just walk to from Africa.

But they're also all places that remained devoid of people for at least 45,000 years after the first *Homo sapiens* set foot on our shores. North America had no North Americans until about 12,000 years ago; South America no South Americans until a squidge after that. The evidence even suggests that Madagascar – just a short sail from southern Africa, where *Homo sapiens* evolved – didn't see a single human being until 11,000 BCE.

And it's worth remembering that the ancestors of Australia's Indigenous peoples were not just the first Australians, they were the first Asians as well. They seemed to have trekked through South-East Asia at least 24,000 years before the arrival of those people whose descendants mostly live there today.

When it came to exploration, in other words, the first Australians were not just ahead of the game, they were essentially the ones who invented it. The first time that someone sailed to our continent and thought 'this looks okay' was not just a big moment for him, her or them. It was a big moment for all human history.

So – to return to our question – how on earth did they get there? Part of the answer is clearly: with time. We're probably talking about a hike that took hundreds of years (much like that time my friends made me walk Wilsons Prom). But the day must have come when these people hit a big southern ocean and realised that they could hike no more. It probably would have taken many generations more to invent a boat capable of tackling short journeys and develop the skills that were needed to sail it.

But hang on a second. Australia isn't a short journey. Even if you're flying first class and have too many sleeping pills, a flight from Singapore, Bangkok or Jakarta still tends to feel very long. Here's where the second part of the answer comes in. They may not have had to sail all that far.

For a little while there, you see, about 60,000 years ago, the world was a chillier place. This meant that we had a lot more ice in the North and South Poles and a lot less water sploshing about in the oceans. A fact that in turn meant the world had more land. Australia, for example, was about 25 per cent bigger than it is today, and Tasmania was (alas) part of the mainland. You could walk there from Uluru if that was your thing.

And by the same token, you could walk north to Papua New Guinea. And from the northern banks of PNG you could see hundreds and hundreds of tiny little islands that have long since been submerged by sea.

We'll never know for sure, but there's a good chance that the original Australians were able to use said islands as stepping stones as they sailed ever further southwards from Asia, seeking further places to fish. Professor Geoffrey Blainey is not a historian that I much like to quote, what with him being a racist old windbag, but he's probably right to suggest that Australia was 'merely the chance terminus of a series of voyages and migrations' carried out over hundreds of years.

But still we're talking about a 'chance terminus' that was a long way away – maybe even a terminus so far away that it was only chanced upon once. Recent studies of mitochondrial DNA suggest that it's entirely possible that Australia's Indigenous population could all be descended from as few as seventy-two people.

Seventy-two people with the singular good fortune to set sail near the end of an ice age. An ice age that literally melted away into water, causing ocean levels to rise about 80 metres and create the much-harder-to-get-to continent we all know today.

Seventy-two people who had the place all to themselves.

Lucky to Be British?

How this book could have been written in Dutch

'You never know what worse luck your bad luck
has saved you from.'
Cormac McCarthy, US writer

Trust. Communication. Regular vacuuming. Quality time together and a lot more apart. A successful marriage has many vital ingredients.

But for me the main one may well be Google Maps. In the days before iPhones could tell us where to drive, long car trips with my partner to somewhere far away were always a highway to hell. Jenny has all the navigational skill of a not-that-bright blindfolded person who's just had a knock to the head. And strictly between you and me, it's possible that I am just as bad. And even worse at keeping an eye on the petrol. Anyway, let's just say that several late-night arguments have taken place on several dark, lonely roadsides that one can't quite find on the map. Hurtful words have been said.

Happy holidays have been ruined. And I maintain I've been right, every time.

My broader point, however, is that navigation is hard. So Captain Cook probably deserves his great fame for managing to get to Australia.

But without a big chunk of luck, he might never have left it. The *Endeavour* might still be lying at the bottom of the Great Barrier Reef, a broken wreck forgotten by history, its brave captain at best a footnote.

Cape Tribulation, you see, was given that name by Cook because his time there proved quite a trial. Sailing 12 kilometres off the coast of what we now call Queensland while on his way home from Botany Bay, the master navigator navigated his way onto a high coral reef. Completely stuck and unable to move on a stormy night with approaching monsoons, Cook ordered his crew to throw 50 tons of supplies overboard in an effort to make the ship lighter.

Freedom finally came when the tide rose – but it came with a problem, in the form of a hole. 'This was an alarming and I may say terrible circumstance,' Cook later wrote in his journal, 'and threatened immediate destruction to us as soon as the Ship was afloat.'

With water flooding in fast, and the shore still 12 kilometres away, that should really have been that for the *Endeavour*. It really shouldn't have been seen again, except by fish and the occasional snorkeler. But Cook's crew survived because of a small lump of coral. A small lump of coral that somehow broke off from the reef, or got sucked up into the hole, and briefly provided a sort of small, makeshift plug.

Granted a tiny window of time, the desperate sailors were able to reinforce the plug with some sails, 'dung' and wool, empty out whatever water they could, and slowly make it to Cape Tribulation. Cook was forced to spend almost two months ashore, carefully mending the ship, near two mountains he named 'Misery' and 'Sorrow'.

'Misery' and 'sorrow' may also be good words to describe a great deal of what happened next: the colonisation of Australia. After 50,000-plus years of having the place to themselves, Indigenous peoples suddenly had to share it with tuberculosis and influenza and measles and smallpox and rapey, murderous land-thieves with prisons and rifles.

But I suppose you could say that it was pretty good luck for the British. Particularly given that Australia could easily have been colonised by someone else long before.

Long before the 'Age of Discovery' – the three centuries or so from about 1492 in which European countries 'found', mapped and conquered a huge chunk of the world – China was all set to do something similar. Much more economically advanced than the West, and well ahead in terms of cannons and guns, 15th-century China also had the world's biggest collection of very big ships. Decades before, when Columbus crossed the Atlantic in the *Santa María*, the Ming Dynasty was building ships more than six times that size. Under the command of an ambitious eunuch called Admiral Zheng, this vast 'Treasure Fleet' was routinely sailing as far as Africa, India and Turkey to buy, sell and trade.

How long would it have been until China sent a fleet south? Probably not too long at all. But in an act of self-destruction rather reminiscent of Brexit, or the time Tony Abbott made himself the minister for women, 16th-century Emperor Zhu Gaochi ordered that the entire fleet be dismantled and burnt, and that all foreign trade would hence-forth be banned. Motivated by xenophobia, as best we can tell, it was a decision that did Chinese merchants zero favours but was certainly good news for the British.

The British could have been beaten by the Portuguese or the Dutch. Both of those powers, after all, took over land in South-East Asia, just a squidge to our north, several centuries before the First Fleet.

So why was Australia not swallowed up by these empires? In the case of Portugal, the simple answer seems to be that they didn't realise that it existed. While that country's traders were in Timor-Leste from 1515 – i.e. just 700 kilometres or so to our north – none of them ever seemed to think it worth venturing south in search of more spices to trade. By the time it was discovered that a big continent was down here, their ability to colonise had well and truly waned, thanks to growing competition from the English and Dutch. It was all they could do to hang on to bits of Indonesia. Any kind of further conquest was completely out of the question.

The Dutch, meanwhile, *did* know it was here. And they knew it a long time before anyone else in Europe. The first European to set foot in the great southern land, after all, was a Dutch navigator named Willem Janszoon. He was followed by a second Dutchman,

Dirk Hartog, in 1616, and at least a dozen more in the decades that followed.

But luckily for the people living here, none of them liked what they saw. Instead of seeing a lush, green land filled with spices and gold, and rich black soil in need of windmills and tulips, Dutch visitors mostly set their clogged feet in the WA desert – and saw sweet fuck-all to make them want to return.

'On this Voyage nothing hath been discovered which can be any way serviceable to the [Dutch East Indies] Company,' wrote one critic, Willem de Vlamingh, in 1694. 'The Soil of this Country hath been found very barren, and as a Desert; no Fresh-water Rivers have been found.' Much like a Yelp reviewer with way too much time on his hands, he also found space to mention our 'small and miserable Trees', 'Millions of Flies' and the way our 'Coast is very foul and full of Rocks.'

Abel Tasman also 'found nothing profitable' in Tasmania, the place that later adopted his name – just 'poor naked people walking along the beaches; without rice or many fruits'. Jan Carstensz similarly had nothing positive to say about this 'arid and poor tract of land without any fruit tree or anything useful to man'.

These are not, I guess, words that we much like to hear. But they may well be words that spared us from wearing clogs.

The Lucky Fleet

How the First Fleet's survival was a bit of a fluke

'In history books, luck is always underplayed and the talent of individuals is usually overplayed.'

Dominic Cummings, former advisor to Boris Johnson

Australia is a great place in all sorts of ways. We have beautiful beaches. We have wonderful wineries. Rupert Murdoch is no longer a citizen and Mel Gibson mostly lives overseas.

But let's all be real here folks. We still have our fair share of problems. Karl Stefanovic can still be seen on TV; Kyle and Jackie O can still be heard on the airwaves. The Gold Coast is yet to be torn down and bulldozed. The people who run Qantas are still to be shot.

But the biggest problem of all, for the less Murdochy among us, is that 26 January is still our national day. I mean, *really*? The First Fleet? What in hell is that all about? Other countries celebrate good stuff on their national days – they mark major revolutions, massive military triumphs; long-sought ends to tyranny or some foreign rule. We, on the other hand, celebrate the *start* of foreign rule. We celebrate a day that a bunch of pasty-white Brits came to a place that had been lived on for thousands of years, and declared that from here on it would be a big prison.

The 26 January 1788 has rightly been renamed 'Invasion Day' by many. But when you consider all the people who died in its wake, you could just as easily call it 'Smallpox Day'. Or 'Measles Day'. Or 'Endless Deadly Strains of Influenza Day'. Not to mention 'Murder and Massacre Day'.

And let's not forget that it was not necessarily all that great a day, either, for the 700 convicts aboard. They were, after all, arriving at a prison. A place where they were going to labour for years, under a hot, beating sun, while wearing chains and getting whipped with a lash. A place with no possibility of escape. A place where they would pray for sweet, sweet death, and probably get it before very long.

The First Fleet's a grim story, however you slice it. But in some ways, it was also a lucky story, because things could actually have been even worse.

For one thing, it could have been 'La Première Flotte'. This whole freaking country could well have been French. We could have been eating snails and smoking Gitanes and surrendering every time someone says the word 'war'. For all their mushy peas and gloominess and Susan Boyle albums, the English at least brought Australia a level of peace and stability – not to mention a political system that was on the path to democracy. The France of 1788, on the other hand, was an absolutist monarchy that was just about to be overthrown by violence. A violent revolution that would be followed by two more violent revolutions over the next fifty-one years – a period that also featured Robespierre's Reign of Terror, Napoleon's bloody dictatorship and a long and unsuccessful war against half of Europe.

This was not a country that I would want to be part of. *Je ne regrette rien*, as Édith Piaf might say.

So how close did Australia get to being L'Australie? The answer, it turns out, is 'very'. A little-remarked fact about the original Australia Day is that First Fleet didn't arrive on its own. Just six days after the convicts turned up, they were joined by two heavily armed frigates (filled with trees, plants, seeds and tools) under the command of Admiral Jean-François de Galaup, comte de La Pérouse. A portly aristocrat with panache and elan (not to mention savoir faire and a certain je ne sais quoi), he had been sent here by Louis XVI as part of a round-the-world voyage to find a few new colonies to add to the pile.

What's more, he was running late! La Pérouse had been supposed to get here in late 1787. The only thing that prevented a French flag from being planted in Botany Bay – and all the territorial disputes that would have promptly ensued – was that La Pérouse was told about some (entirely mythical) 'treasure islands' while sailing through the Pacific and took a long detour to find them.

Had he stuck to schedule, writers like Margaret Cameron-Ash believe, Australia's history would have been 'very different'. England

and France were, after all, just four years from their last war and less than five from their next one. Relations were, shall we say, a bit chilly. 'Although we can argue that the British had eleven ships and the French had only two, don't forget half the people on these ships were convicts and totally unarmed ... So I don't think [First Fleet leader Arthur] Phillip would have stood much chance.'

In the event, no shots were fired at the time. But there was certainly no guarantee that France wouldn't return, guns a-blazing, once La Pérouse got back to Paris to report on his findings. He did, after all, stick around what became Sydney for more than six weeks.

Time that he did not spend eating hors d'oeuvre, having ménages à trois or making double entendres to some femme fatale. Time that he instead spent methodically surveying Sydney's coastline and writing a report on whether it could serve as a colony.

What was in that report? And, more to the point, what would the French king have done when he saw it? As luck would have it, we will never know, because La Pérouse and his crew didn't make it back to Paris before 1789's French Revolution – a revolution that led the colony-hungry king to lose all of his power. And, a little later, all his head.

In fact, La Pérouse and his crew didn't make it back at all. Their fate was only discovered decades later, when the broken remains of two French frigates were found on the ocean floor not too far from what are now called the Solomons.

Had they returned to Paris in time with a favourable report about the great southern land, would we have seen war in Sydney? It's possible of course, but as writer and ABC broadcaster Michael Cathcart points out, the more likely outcome is that the French would have just created a second little colony somewhere else on the Australian coast. 'The colonisation of a country the size of Australia by [only] one country was so against the odds and so improbable it is unlikely to happen again.'

'Australia,' agrees *Quadrant*'s Leo Maglen, 'could easily have been not a single nation, but one divided into competing European colonies, with all the likelihood of frontier disputes and inter-colonial wars.... Not having to share a land border with another nation has bestowed upon us huge benefits.'

But of course, it also made for huge challenges. The second role played by luck in the story of the First Fleet lies in the fact that most of the people aboard more or less managed to survive.

It's worth keeping in mind that this was a pretty major undertaking. There are much, much easier and cheaper ways of housing a few hundred convicts than on a 25,000 kilometre journey through mostly unchartered waters and every extreme of weather. 'Never before,' journalist Michael Crowley reminds us, 'had so many people been moved so far on the face of the Earth.'

What's more, the move was organised in minimal time and with little input from experts. The British East India Company had the logistical experience to plan such a journey, but they weren't involved. When the First Fleet set off from Portsmouth in May 1787, not a single person aboard had ever seen the Pacific, and only one was armed with a device designed to help them gauge latitude – i.e.

actually know where they were. And if the surviving diary entries from those aboard provide any guide, they also seem to have set off just in time for 252 days of truly terrible weather. For 252 days of 'violent storms', 'huge swells' and constant 'severe winds'. Not to mention 'rough seas' and 'snow'.

'I never before saw a sea in such a rage,' wrote ship's surgeon Arthur Bowes Smyth, though it turned out that he soon would again. 'The sky blackened, the wind arose and in half an hour more it blew a perfect hurricane, accompanied with thunder, lightning and rain ... Every other ship in the fleet ... sustained some damage ... during the storm. The convict women in our ship were so terrified that most of them were down on their knees at prayers.'

'Just as we had dined,' runs another typical diary entry, 'a most tremendous sea broke in at the weather scuttle of the great cabin and ran with a great stream all across the cabin, and as the door of my cabin happened not to be quite closed shut the water half-filled it, the sheets and the blankets being all on a flow.' Clearly not a man with much use for the comma, he also noted that, 'The water ran from the quarterdeck nearly into the great cabin and struck against the main and missen chains with such a force as at first alarmed us all greatly but particularly me as I believed [the] ship was drove in pieces.'

So, all things considered, the First Fleet was also the lucky fleet. It's really something of a miracle that all eleven ships not only managed to locate Botany Bay, but managed to safely anchor half a kilometre off its shore, with the loss of just forty-eight passengers.

But it's a safe bet that Captain Phillip might have wished that he was one of them after he got on a little boat, rowed to the shore and took a look at the land that awaited him. Bottom line: it was a bit of a shithole. Almost bad enough to make you wish you were back in England.

While Captain Cook had spent a week at Botany Bay some eighteen years earlier, he had not, it appeared, spent all that much time thinking about whether it was a place where lots of people could live. It took less than a day for Phillip to realise that Botany Bay was far too shallow and windy to provide a safe harbour for ships, and that the land around it was more or less a big swamp. Instead of lush, fragrant meadows with thick trees for timber, and rich, black soil where the fleet could plant lots of crops, he saw sand, clay and mud, thick swarms of mosquitos, and next to nothing in the way of fresh water.

What to do? I myself would have panicked and just given up at this point, what with 1500 starving, sick passengers still stuck offshore in small, battered ships, being tossed around by storms, winds and swells. Supplies were low. Morale was lower. Television had not yet been invented.

But Captain Phillip was made of stern stuff. La Pérouse might have called it sangfroid. Instead of curling up into a foetal position and rubbing his face while he moaned softly and shed bitter tears, our hero took out a copy of Captain Cook's diary. 'There appeared to be safe anchorage,' Cook had written, not too far away from Bot Bay, in between two rocky headlands that his ship had sailed past.

Phillip dispatched a ship north to investigate. And 'had the satisfaction of finding' what he later described as 'the finest harbour in the world' was a mere 15 kilometres up the coast.

Still, that did not mean that getting to what he called 'Sydney Cove' would be easy. With violent headwinds battering Botany Bay, it was only 'with the utmost difficulty and danger [and] with many hairbreadth escapes [that we] got out of the harbour's mouth', reported Arthur Bowes Smyth. 'It was next to a miracle that some of the ships were not lost, the danger was so very great.'

'We should have gone to pieces in less than half of an hour,' concurred Lieutenant Ralph Clark, of the Royal Marines. 'If it had not been by the greatest good luck, we should have been both on the shore [and] on the rocks, and the ships must have been all lost, and the greater part, if not the whole on board drowned.'

So on 26 January 1788 – a full eight days after Phillip set foot on our shores – he disembarked once again onto what is now Circular Quay and announced the launch of a new British colony. He dutifully thanked God and King George for granting him the privilege to serve in their glorious name – and probably continued to thank them right up until 1792, when he was finally allowed to quit and get the fuck back to England.

But he should have been thanking his lucky stars instead for the fact that he still had an actual colony to abandon. The First Fleet was incredibly lucky to survive those four years. It's a minor miracle that they didn't all die from famine. As ANU climate scientist Dr Joëlle Gergis points out:

When the British sailed into Australian waters, they had no idea of what awaited them ... HMS *Endeavour* had only briefly skirted past modern-day Sydney Harbour in May 1770, so the British knew next to nothing of the land, its climate or its people. Perhaps they expected that life would resemble their other colonial outposts like India, or an undeveloped version of England.

Needless to say, it did not.

While Sydney was a perfect place to dock a few ships, and super close to lots of fresh, running water, it was at the time not a great place to farm. For one thing, the soil was covered in rocks (hence the name of Australia's first suburb: 'The Rocks'). And for another, it had heaps of huge and hard trees, which quickly blunted the small and soft English axes. And things didn't get that much better once said trees were cut down and torn from the ground: the would-be farmers were left with an arid and sandy, dry soil that was patently unsuited to European-style crops. Crops that were also not a great idea to plant in February, right at the height of the hot southern summer. Most of the few seeds that took root most were eaten by ants and mice, and most of the sheep were devoured by dingos.

At least, they said to themselves, they had the cattle ... until one dark night when the colony's entire herd escaped into the bush.

Not only was Sydney a crap place to farm, the job was being attempted by some truly crap farmers. While the First Fleet had brought plenty of marines, sailors and bureaucrats along to oversee the 700 people in chains, it was rather light on for people who actually knew what a plough was, let alone how to actually use one.

The convicts were no real help at all, since they were mostly from England's overcrowded cities. They knew how to pick a pocket or two, but that was about as far as their useful skills went. And even with the best will and all the skill in the world, many of this would-be labour force would have been simply incapable of hard manual labour after spending so many months at sea: so many damp, dark days chained up below deck, one hundred in each disease-riddled hovel. Days of clutching their empty stomachs as the sea heaved and lurched, surrounded by rats and maggots and weevils and mice and people with thick cockney accents.

By the time all but one ship had gone back to Blighty, the colony's food situation was starting to look pretty dire. But at least it had a few years' worth of barley and wheat, which the First Fleet had brought by the sackful ...

No, actually. Check that. Thanks to an unexpected influx of weevils, plus sea water and the summer heat, most of that turned out to be completely inedible. In fact, Phillip calculated that the colony had less than a year's worth of food. Maybe forty-nine weeks' worth, if they were careful with rations.

So, where were we? Oh yes, the word 'dire'. Not such a bad one for the situation. Captain Watkin Tench wrote a few more:

> Famine was approaching with gigantic strides, and gloom and dejection overspread every countenance ... All our labour and attention were turned

> on one subject – the procuring of food ... The insufficiency of our ration soon diminished our execution of labour. Both soldiers and convicts pleaded such loss of strength, as to find themselves unable to perform their accustomed tasks.

The Second Fleet had been supposed to make things better, but somehow managed to make them worse. Famously dubbed the 'Death Fleet', the ships that arrived in 1790 were meant to bring more supplies, more seeds, more animals, more tools and more able-bodied men who actually knew how to use them. Instead, they brought black gums and purple limbs, loose teeth and broken bones. Not to mention dysentery, starvation, lice, scurvy and a slight blow to morale.

'The misery I saw amongst them is indescribable,' reported Reverend Richard Johnson about the 750 or so convicts that survived the disastrous voyage (more than 250 had died on the way). Pale, emaciated and mostly unclothed, they were

> wretched, naked, filthy, dirty, louzy ... unable to stand, to creep, or even to stir hand or foot ... Upon their being brought up to the open air some fainted, some died upon deck, and others in the boat before they reached the shore ... some creeped upon their hands and knees, and some were carried upon the backs of others.

More than half were immediately hospitalised. A quarter were dead within weeks. This was not, in short, the fresh, new and vibrant workforce that the starving colony so desperately needed. This was a fresh, new and vibrant drain on their dwindling supplies.

Australia needed help if it was to see out 1790.

But don't worry, help was well on the way. Two ships, the HMS *Guardian* and the HMS *Sirius*, were soon due to arrive with all sorts of vital supplies.

Or rather, do worry. Because the *Guardian*, and its heaving stronghold of cattle, sheep, seeds and fruit trees, somehow managed to crash into an iceberg two weeks out from the Cape of Good Hope. Most of the crew made it out of the wreck in one piece, but the same can't be said for nearly all of their cargo.

And the *Sirius*, it seemed, was in equally good hands ... insofar as it managed to hit a reef near Norfolk Island and sink in full view of the shore. In Colonel David Collins's not especially snappy words: 'The general melancholy which prevailed in this settlement when the above unwelcome intelligence was made public need not be described.'

Ralph Clark, however, was happy to describe it. 'Gracious God what will become of us all,' wrote that cheerful optimist. 'The whole of our provisions in the ship, now a wreck before us. I hope in God that we will be able to save some if not all but why do I flatter myself with such hopes – there is at present no prospect except that of starving.'

By now, the desperate colony's 'only remaining hope' rested in what was by now its only remaining ship – a tiny, leaky, worn-out little brig appropriately enough called the HMS *Supply*. Phillip sent it away to the closest town to find what it could ... even though the closest town was a six-month sail. Tench wrote in his diary: 'The *Supply* left for Batavia, carrying with her fervent prayers for her safety, and an anxious population watched her out of sight.'

Come October 1790, they were all still watching anxiously for the *Supply* – and, wouldn't you know it, the ship came into view. And it had not just lived up to its name and brought a few months' worth of supplies, it had miraculously managed to persuade a random Dutch ship to bring up the rear. The 300-tonne *Waakzaamheid* arrived three weeks later carrying 383 barrels of beef, pork and flour, 454 kilograms of sugar and 32 tonnes of rice.

Just enough to keep the colony up and running until the following year, when a La Niña came along, bringing with it some much-needed rain.

Just enough rain to turn their fortunes around.

Just enough rain to create a place called Australia.

Medical Miracles

Cures and procedures that were invented by accident

'Some say that laughter is the best medicine. Obviously, they have yet to try medicine.'

Unknown

On 17 November 1961, a young Sydney woman named Veronica Hopson was sent home to die. Suffering from a particularly acute form of blood cancer, which had also burrowed its way into her bones, the fervent Catholic had been given 'perhaps a month to live' and decided that she would rather spend it away from the hospital, and close to God, praying with a local order of nuns.

Kathleen Evans took much the same tack in 1993, after an inoperable and fast-moving cancer was found to have spread through her brain and her lungs. Given, once again, just a few weeks to live, the lifelong smoker got hold of a suitable relic (some fabric from a famous nun's tunic) and put her faith in the power of prayer.

Both women got better. Swiftly. Fully. Miraculously. Inexplicably. And it was all thanks to Mary MacKillop. Though she had died around a hundred years earlier, that much-revered Australian nun had been the owner of the tunic that Evans had clung to each night, and she had been the founder of the order with whom Hopson had prayed.

Both of these medical miracles were later declared to be just that – miracles – by the exacting scientific minds that run Vatican City. Actual, bona fide, God-given miracles which meant that 'the blessed Mary' became Australia's first saint. Hallelujah. Praise the Lord. Etc.

Be that as it may, non-supernatural explanations are also available. Maybe both women were misdiagnosed?

Or maybe they both just got lucky. 'Medical miracles', after all, are not quite as rare as the phrase might suggest. Turn on the news any night of the week, and chances are you'll see someone who's just woken up, compos mentis, from a six-month-long coma, or a blind person who's somehow got back their sight. I myself know a two-packs-a-day man who's still going strong in his nineties and has never prayed a day in his life. (I'm pretty sure I could beat him in a fight. But I'd fight dirty, just to be extra sure.) None of them, as far as I know, have got a piece of nun tunic.

Anyway, my point is that these things don't come down to piety. Like so much else, they just come down to luck.

Australian media tycoon Kerry Packer, for example, was a long way from Christ-like – but just like Jesus, he came back from the dead.

'I've been to the other side, mate,' the rapacious media mogul once reflected, 'and there is nothing there. The good news is there's no devil. The bad news is there's no heaven.' Not unlike the devil himself, though without the looks or charisma, Packer suffered a heart attack during a 1990 polo match which left him clinically dead for more than six minutes. And dead is exactly how he should have stayed, were it not for two strokes of luck. (1) An ambulance just happened to be passing by. And (2) it happened to be one of the very, very few ambulances in Sydney that was equipped with a portable defibrillator. As Packer put it, 'How lucky was I?'

Perhaps a better question, though, is, 'How lucky are all of us?' Because for all that the average doctor doesn't mind keeping you waiting, and is always happy to charge a small fortune, they are in one small but very important respect very different to the doctors of yore.

The difference is this: they are not trying to kill you.

As British historian Professor David Wootton argues in his book *Bad Medicine*, from the time of the ancient Greeks until about the 1910s (when a strange new 'germ theory' gave us antibiotics), most medicines not only failed to cure people, they did a whole lot to make them sick.

Got leukaemia, for example? Then why not try arsenic? It was the standard 'cure' for it until the 1920s, and was also used to fight asthma and heartburn. Sufferers of constipation, meanwhile, were often advised to try mercury, and men who couldn't get it up were advised to sip radium. For nagging pain, Victorian doctors would prescribe cocaine – or, after 1898, the Bayer Company's Heroin©. Come down with cholera? Why not try getting electrocuted? Mentally ill? How's about a lobotomy?

Put in that context, pretty much everything that you can buy at your chemist today can be classified as a 'medical miracle'. You and I are lucky to live in an age of careful research and scientific rigour. An age where medical procedures rarely, if ever, involve unicorn's horns, or sacrificing a virgin underneath a full moon. Australians born today can expect to live decades longer than Australians born centuries ago, and the majority of us can expect to spend most of that time feeling pretty good and pain-free.

But terms like 'miracle' may be even more apt when you're talking about medical procedures that were created by luck. About modern-day cures that, yes, owe a bit to scientific rigour and careful research, but that would probably not be around, curing people today, were it not for some kind of strange accident.

Take Valium, for example: the anti-anxiety pill that helped 1950s housewives to cope with the fact that they had 1950s husbands. *I Love Lucy* could only fill so many hours in the day, after all, and many women probably didn't love her that much. Also able to help with alcohol withdrawal (or, if you preferred, really spark up a sherry), 'mother's little helper' was certainly invented as a result of careful research. But it was careful research into a new kind of clothes dye. Valium started out as an attempt to answer the question: is there a faster way to turn fabric purple?

The first anaesthetic, by the same token, had nothing to do with numbing pain when it was invented in 1772. Properly known as nitrous oxide, laughing gas was just one of many chemical compounds that a part-time chemist, Joseph Priestley, just happened to come up with, in between writing weighty books about theology, politics and the correct use of grammar. Just like his other contributions to knowledge, it was largely ignored, because it was complicated and had no clear use. If laughing gas was used at all in those early days, it was just for an occasional laugh at a very small and select group of upper-class parties. Its ability to kill pain remained unknown ... until the day of a Mayfair ball. The story goes that some well-born fop took a giggly mouthful of gas before treading the boards for a waltz or cotillion. Somehow he then managed cut himself badly, drenching the dancefloor with blood ... but continued to boogie, completely oblivious, unaware of the injury and unaffected by pain.

Dr Georgios Papanicolaou was also completely oblivious to the fact that he was about to save millions of lives when he woke up one winter's day in 1925. A researcher at Cornell University, he had been spending his time studying the sex chromosomes of female guinea pigs by getting a sample of their vaginal fluid. Exactly why, I couldn't tell you – I guess we all have our little hobbies – but it was apparently something to do with mammalian reproduction. Anyway, after a few years of smearing said fluid on a little glass slide, then popping it under a microscope, he decided to expand his studies to other mammalian reproducers, including a few female humans.

It just so happened that one of the women who had contributed a sample was, unbeknown to her, suffering from uterine cancer. We only know this because, to his total astonishment, Papanicolaou found that he could see her cancer cells on the little slide. He had quite accidentally invented a quick and easy test for uterine cancer's early detection. 'The first observation of cancer cells in the smear of the uterine cervix,' he later wrote, 'gave me one of the greatest thrills I ever experienced during my scientific career.'

While they're not quite as quick or cheap as a Pap smear, X-rays are every bit as effective when it comes to finding problems the naked eye cannot see. And its invention owes every bit as much to good luck. Back in the 1890s, a Prussian mechanical engineer named Wilhelm Röntgen conducted all sorts of experiments with cathode ray tubes to prove something or other about electricity or light. Precisely what, I really can't tell you, but the point is that revolutionising medicine was pretty much the furthest thing from his mind. He would have spent more time watching soldiers goosestep and wondering if he was getting too old to wear tight leather pants. But then came the day when Röntgen noticed a green ray of light was somehow leaking out from one of the cardboard-covered tubes and causing weird shapes to appear on a platinobarium screen about 9 feet away. He called this an 'X ray' because he had no idea what it was. The 'X' was intended to be a placeholder.

Even luckier, in a sense, was one Wilson Greatbatch (though this run of luck clearly didn't extend to his name). A self-described 'humble tinkerer' from New York State, Greatbatch was humbly tinkering with a heart-rate monitor back in 1956, simply because it was broken and he'd offered to fix it. But just like the plumber who keeps on 'fixing' my tap, Greatbatch's skills were not quite up to scratch. Reaching into a box full of tiny components for a brown, black and orange resistor, he accidentally pulled out a brown, black and *green* one. A resistor that contained 1000 kiloohms (whatever the hell they are) rather than the 10 kiloohms the broken monitor required.

The monitor should have been damaged beyond repair (much like my tap), but instead something quite strange occurred. It started to emit an electrical pulse. A slow, steady series of electrical thumps that sounded a lot like a healthy heartbeat. 'I stared at the thing in disbelief,' the thirty-seven-year-old wrote many years later, 'and then realized that this was exactly what was needed to drive a heart.' He had accidentally created a pacemaker.

Want some more medicines that were essentially invented though luck? Well, as luck would have it, I have quite a few.

Viagra, for example, was designed to improve blood flow by 'relaxing' the blood vessels around our hearts, combating heart disease. Botox was supposed to treat muscle spasms in eyelids.

Want some more? Well, sure. But if you're a dog lover, you're not going to like it.

In 1889, two German physicians decided that a good way to study the role of the pancreas in digestion would be to remove one from a dog ... while it was still alive ... and then continue to water and feed it.

As grotesque and awful experiments go, this was right up there with Russell Crowe's singing career and the recent remake of *Dirty Dancing*.

Anyway, a few days into all of this awfulness, Joseph von Mering and Oskar Minkowski noticed something a little odd about their lab floor. Swarms of flies kept landing on the dog's little puddles of urine – as far as they could tell, so as to have a drink. This would not have been particularly odd if the dog had had diabetes, a disease that causes the body to secrete sugar in pee. But the doctors had examined the dog carefully before cutting it up and knew for sure that this had not been the case. Conclusion? By removing the pancreas, they had accidentally *given* the dog diabetes. Diabetes remains a major issue today, but thanks to those flies, we more or less know how to manage it. One in twenty Australians live with it today but most don't find it such a big stress.

Stress, on the other hand, is a very big stress. Anxiety is a huge cause of all kinds of health problems. So if you're constantly worrying about cancer or heart disease ... then, well, maybe you ought to be. Which is a worry, I know.

But there's probably no need to stress that your stress will cause stomach ulcers. Or really, to stress about ulcers at all. For one thing, they are much rarer these days – and for another, most can quickly be cured. Forty years ago, however, stomach ulcers were a chronic and extremely common condition – a disease with frequent relapses that used to plague about one in ten Aussies, and ultimately kill quite a few. Ulcers meant a constant risk of a deadly infection, or some form of internal bleeding. Especially ulcer-prone patients did not just face a life full of pain, they faced the prospect of having their stomach removed, because gastric ulcers could often turn cancerous.

So what changed? The short answer is that two perfectly ordinary doctors from Perth completely revolutionised how we see the disease. Back in the 1970s, you see, the received medical wisdom was that stomach ulcers were actually all in the head – i.e. that they were caused by stress. Early stage patients were by and large told to worry a bit less, lay off the alcohol and maybe avoid spicy food ... right up until the time that they duly got cancer. Nowadays, however, they are given antibiotics. And, a week after that, they are cured. That's because we know now that ulcers aren't caused by stress, they're caused by *Helicobacter pylori*. Found in every second stomach (it may or may not 'move in' when you're a kid), these screw-shaped bacteria are usually problem-free tenants, just like the trillions of other little microbes and bacteria that float about in our bodies. Occasionally, they cause ulcers and need to be killed with antibiotics. But mostly you wouldn't know they were there.

Which may help to explain exactly why we *didn't* know they were there, right up until the late 1970s. The accepted medical wisdom was that it wasn't even possible for bacteria to exist in a healthy stomach, because healthy stomachs are full of acid that would kill them stone-dead. Australian doctor Barry Marshall explained it:

> Nobody ever looked for bacteria in [a healthy] stomach, and any that were seen there were thought to result from contamination [of the

sample]. People who had seen them had always washed them off to look at the stomach cells underneath, and just ignored the bacteria stuck all over the surface.

Marshall's colleague Robin Warren, however, was a man with a hobby. A pathologist with no particular interest in stomach ulcers, Warren loved to spend his spare time with a microscope looking at stray hunks of diseased human flesh. Which, as hobbies go, may be a touch on the creepy side. Or at least not the sort of thing that people look for on Tinder. But in 1979, it was a hobby that led him to see something odd: the same sort of (weird, screw-shaped) bacteria kept on popping up, again and again, on samples from patients with stomach problems. He wrote to the local hospital, suggesting the strange puzzle be investigated. But his suggestion was politely ignored.

A couple of years later, a young intern called Barry Marshall was doing a six-month elective in gastroenterology and needed some kind of research project to pass the class.

> I had a number of different possibilities, but, as a fluke, my boss showed me a letter from Robin Warren saying, basically, 'We've got twenty patients with bacteria in their stomach, where you shouldn't have bacteria living ... Is there a doctor in gastroenterology who wants to work with me on this and find out what's wrong with these people?'

Marshall came aboard because he 'thought it would be fun'. (Doctors are weird. But anyway, we move on.) 'We were not looking for the cause of ulcers,' he said. 'We just wanted to find out what these bacteria were. We were saying, "Maybe this happens only in Perth. Maybe this is Australian, and you catch the bacteria from kangaroos or wombats or quokkas."'

A few dozen samples later, however, the pair became convinced that the bacteria *was* causing ulcers. What they now had to do was convince the medical world, by cultivating some *Helicobacter pylori* from scratch in a lab and seeing what would happen when it went in a tum. The only problem was that the bacteria was proving impossible to cultivate. The pair spent months and months putting agar plates in an incubator, to absolutely no avail. What they needed was a stroke of luck.

Which, of course, was what they got. It came in the form of a four-day weekend. Just before the Easter holidays in 1982, a staff member at Perth Hospital got into the holiday spirit just a little too early. He had been supposed to remove the latest set of agar plates from the incubator, to confirm that yet again nothing had grown on them, then throw them out and insert a few more. This was because, by that point, the plates would have been there for two days: the amount of incubation time standard practice required. But this young slacker buggered off to the beach instead, which meant that the agar plates accidentally stayed in the incubator an extra few days. And I think you can guess what they grew.

The lab techs had been throwing the cultures out after two days because with strep, on the first day we may see something, but by the second day it's covered with contamination and you might as well throw it in the bin. That was the mentality of the lab: anything that didn't grow in two days didn't exist. But, they discovered, *Helicobacter* is slow.

Marshall's next step was to drink some himself, to see what it did to his then-healthy tum.

As luck would have it, he soon had an ulcer. Along with a shiny, new Nobel Prize.

PART TWO

CHEATING DEATH

Have you ever wondered why it's considered 'bad luck' to break a mirror? Frankly, for most people, it would seem more like good luck, what with ignorance being bliss and all that. I myself haven't really enjoyed looking in one of the things since my last good hair day, way back in 1994.

It turns out that the answer is fairly straightforward. Back in ye olde times, people used to believe that their reflection might well contain a small part of their soul, so they very naturally took care not to break it.

What about it being bad luck to let a black cat cross your path? Well, once again, what now seems like a superstition seems to have started out as a perfectly sensible piece of advice. Witches, after all, were known to keep cats. So it was only logical to not want to see one of the things, as it probably meant that a witch was nearby. If you happened to run across a black cat, you might be within easy aim of some kind of hex, curse or spell.

Spilled salt, by the same token, didn't used to bring on 'bad luck' per se but was instead thought to bring on Beelzebub. Exactly why Satan was drawn to salt, I'm not super-clear, but he apparently felt the same way about people who walked under ladders or had anything to do with the number thirteen.

Is there any actual point to these random factoids? Yes, I feel sure that there must be.

Maybe it's that superstitions *are* kind of silly. Unless you truly believe that demonic forces are hovering nearby, and certain practical steps are required to repel then, then there's really no need to avoid stepping on a crack. There's no need to cross your fingers the next time you feel worried, or to do your best to touch wood.

But the bigger point, I think, is that you'll probably do it anyway. Not everyone believes in witches and warlocks and princes of darkness. But most of us believe in not pushing our luck. Because we all know that life can be hell.

Buckley's Chance

Aussies who survived being lost in the outback

'Scientists have calculated that the chances of something so patently absurd actually existing are millions to one. But magicians have calculated that million-to-one chances crop up nine times out of ten.'

Terry Pratchett, UK fantasy writer

Some tourists say that Australia is a little light on for landmarks. That outside of Sydney Harbour, Uluru and ... um ... I don't know, the Big Potato, we don't really have any sights that a tourist simply *must* see: any sights that they simply *have to* take a pic with in order to prove to the world they've been here.

Such tourists are entirely correct. And generally speaking, they're also quite grateful. As any Aussie knows, an overseas holiday to somewhere like Europe can often feel a lot more like hard work. There are just so many sights that you feel you must march to; so many churches, museums and galleries that you must pretend to enjoy. Holidays in Australia require none of that shit. They're about naps, swims and drinks in the sun.

There is, however, an exception to this rule. An exception that goes by the name of 'grey nomad'. A sort of senile subspecies of Australian traveller, easily identified by their thin hair and thick parkas, grey nomads want to track down every single sight that this country contains and seem to believe that we have more than three. Pretty much anything can make a grey nomad's 'must-see' list, be it a beach, rock or hill. It just has to be dull and involve a long drive.

The result is that this genus can be found pretty much everywhere across this wide, brown land, driving very slowly, honking very loudly and taking a long time to fill up their tank. You can see them driving in arid deserts .... across raging rivers ... up snowy mountains ... through snake-filled forests. Essentially, you can see them in every place that no sane person would ever go.

My point here (see, I knew we'd get to it eventually) is that Australia is full of shit that can kill you. It's big and it's dry and it's hot, hot, hot and it's chock-full of spiders and snakes. If grey nomads didn't have campervans, they would have Buckley's chance. By which I mean next to no chance of getting back home alive.

Much like, as it happens, William Buckley. While the phrase 'Buckley's and none' probably comes from Buckley & Nunn, a ye olde Melbourne department store, it's generally associated with the 'wild white man' from northern England who was sent to Australia back in 1803. 'Generally represented as being of low intelligence', this 'tall, ungainly' man may not have been a hit with the ladies, according to an acquaintance by the name of George Russell:

> Altogether his looks were not in his favour; he had a bushy head of black hair, a low forehead with overhanging eyebrows nearly concealing his small eyes, a short snub nose, a face very much marked by smallpox, and was just such a man as one would suppose fit to commit burglary or murder.

It is wrong to judge people by their appearance, of course. But in this instance, George's judgement was right. Convicted of stealing a few bolts of cloth, William Buckley became one of the first prisoners to be sent to what's now Victoria, to a small penal settlement on the south coast. The twenty-three-year-old bricklayer also became one of the first people to escape it when, after a couple of months, he managed to run away in the company of five other convicts.

Or rather, in the company of *four* other convicts, given that one of the escapees was shot within seconds.

After a couple of hot, disorienting days in the bush, the remaining five started to realise that not having any food, water or idea where they were could be a bit of a problem. Hungry, thirsty and terrified of the 'natives', two of them decided to return to the settlement and the sweet relief of handcuffs and floggings.

The week after that saw two more turn back, convinced that their death was nearby. And we can be pretty sure that, in this, they were right, given that they never made it back to the penal settlement, and their bodies were never found.

That just left Buckley to bravely march on, in what he hoped was the direction of Sydney. Employing all the Aussie bushcraft you would expect to see from someone who'd grown up in a large English town, he was 'determined to endure every kind of suffering rather than again surrender my liberty'. And 'every kind of suffering' is what he duly endured.

But then came a day when Buckley's luck changed. A day when – dehydrated, starving, drenched with BO and desperately in need of a new pair of undies – he stumbled across a spear that was stuck in the ground. So he pulled it out, figuring that not only would it help him to catch his next meal, it would probably come in handy when he came face to face with the Indigenous peoples in the area – a day that would surely come soon.

And that day accordingly came, when Buckley was near what we now call Wye River. But it turned out that there was no need for him to start stabbing. Instead, as he later wrote in his memoirs, the locals 'came up and viewed me for some time with evident astonishment [and] at length made signs to me to follow them'.

> I immediately did so although I despaired of my life as my impression was that they intended to kill me ... On reaching a hut or 'Willum' near which was a Waterhole, I made signs that I was thirsty, and they gave me

some water and, without being asked, offered me some gum beat up and prepared in their manner. They then all sat down and a general howling was set up around me, the women crying and sobbing...

What was that all about, you ask. Well, I answer, it turned out that Buckley's spear had not just been sticking out of a random patch of dirt. It had been sticking out of a particular grave. Both the grave and the spear had belonged to Murrangurk, a much-revered Elder. And a much-revered Elder who, much like our Will, had been bearded, tall and ungainly.

When they saw this ghostly white weirdo holding Murrangurk's spear, the locals naturally concluded that he was just that: a ghost, Murrangurk's spirit risen up from the grave. The lucky convict was given food, water, shelter and the warmest of welcomes, instead of being killed in cold blood. He went on to live with the Wathaurong for the next thirty-two years, before finally deciding to move to a new little village called Melbourne and get to work on a memoir.

Now, if Robert Bogucki ever writes a memoir, it's a safe bet that fictional ghosts will get a mention there too. But in his case, that ghost will be God and/or Jesus: two characters who also pop up in the Bible.

A firefighter and furniture remover from rural Alaska who may or may not have been in his right mind, Bogucki was a little religious in the way that Nick Kyrgios is a little obnoxious. In other words, he was extremely religious. Painfully religious. Slappably, turn-off-the-telly religious. Religious in a way that kind of puts you off tennis, and makes you worry about the youth of today.

Anyway, where was I? Oh yes: Robert Bogucki, crazy zealot. Back in 1999, when he turned thirty-three, he decided to follow the example set by Jesus when he turned that age and spend forty days and forty nights all alone in the desert, fasting, praying, renouncing Satan and generally being a teensy bit weird. In June 1999, therefore, Bogucki flew to Broome, then drove 300 kilometres south and abandoned his car.

Not quite registering that the Australian Great Sandy Desert is a great sandy desert, and as such not a place to ride bikes, his plan was to cycle east for three days, until he ran out of food, then set up camp and do his forty-day fast. Once he'd managed to find God, he would get back on the bike and continue on to Fitzroy Crossing. A spiritual journey that, in worldly terms, would cover about 600 kilometres.

'[I was] thinking that would be something that would be a good way to get away from the modern world and all its fakeness,' this deep thinker later explained. 'All the shit that says, "money runs the world" and "bow down to the system" and "be a slave to the system."'

Some systems, however, are broadly worth following. One such system, I would argue, is roads. It took two days for Bogucki to accept that bikes are just not made for endless soft sand ... and make the idiotic decision to trudge on by foot.

Five weeks later, he was trudging still. Over 30 kilograms lighter and, of course, with no idea where he was. 'The food that I had lasted for a few days,' he later told the press. 'Basically after that I couldn't tell you what exactly I was eating – plants, flower-type things.'

As to water, it 'wasn't hard to come by at first, I was coming across billabongs'. But before long he was forced to start digging metre-deep holes to try to suck on damp sand. 'Without water, your brain doesn't kind of do very well. It's kind of like being drunk and trying to do math.'

Geography, it seemed, was also a struggle, with the would-be penitent wandering every which way – except for the direction of Fitzroy Crossing. That made finding him even more of a struggle for the police trackers, volunteers and search-and-rescue teams that spent several weeks combing the Great Sandy Desert – and completely failing to find any trace of him.

So how on earth did he get out alive? Reader, I give you the power of the press. After no less than forty-three days in the heat, our doughty hero was finally spotted. Not by a trained rescue team. And not by a tracker. But by the *A Current Affair* crew. Flying in a Channel 9 helicopter to try to get some dramatic desert footage for their 6.30pm show, the TV crew didn't initially realise that they had found the missing man when they spotted someone from far above.

'His head was down and he didn't react to the helicopter at all, so we naturally assumed he was one of the searchers,' said the pilot.

'When the helicopter flew over, I just kept walking,' the ever-rational Bogucki later explained.

> I didn't stop until he flew around again. I looked up and I thought, 'I think they saw me, what the hell am I going to do now? I haven't talked to anybody for a while and what am I going to say to these people about what I have been doing?' And, of course, all that was blown out of the water when [the helicopter pilot] comes up and says, 'Are you Mr Bogucki?' And that was the end of that. I don't have to say anything. They know who I am and what I have been doing. It slowly all settled in.

Confronted by a gaunt, sunstruck shadow of a man, who was clearly dehydrated and not far from death, the crew naturally sprang into action. They got out their cameras and microphones and tripods and boom poles and spent the next twenty minutes conducting a TV interview – obviously pausing at times to get a good close-up or wide shot, adjust the sound and play around with the lighting. But after that wrapped, they took him more or less straight to a hospital – several camera operators closely in tow. Freedom of the press is a wonderful thing, but it would be nice if we could all find a way to enjoy it while keeping journalists in some kind of dungeon.

But, all things considered, Bogucki still probably got better press treatment than the 'bumbling Brit', a brutally derided British tourist technically called Martin Lake.

Dumber than a box of hair but probably not quite as useful, Lake first hit the headlines in 2006, after taking a stroll in a reserve 4 kilometres from Alice Springs. Ignoring the numerous clearly marked signs urging people to stay on the path, he wandered off it, got lost in the bush and managed to stay lost for more than three days.

Having not thought to bring a hat, let alone sunscreen or water, the fifty-year-old looked like 'freshly cooked lobster' by the time a search team tracked him down. 'I don't think I could have lasted another day out there,' he said of the three freezingly cold nights that had given way to hot days. 'I was on my last legs.'

'I think he was a bit embarrassed about it because he realised that people just don't get lost in that area,' a less-than-discreet hotel receptionist later told reporters, as Lake recuperated in a paid room above. 'He was also aware that he could have easily perished out there because you can't really survive in the midday heat for more than a couple of days without water.'

All's well that ends well, as they say. But as so often happens, they are quite wrong.

After a few more days of seeing the sights in Alice Springs – those sights being four shops and a pub – Lake decided that he should probably revisit that reserve, just outside town, because he never really saw it the first time.

It goes without saying that this time, he knew to stay on the marked path.

And it goes without saying that this time, he didn't. It took five full days of wandering in the bush – five full days in among snakes and spiders, under a burning-hot sun – before Lake finally mustered up the courage to face an even worse fate. He turned on his phone and sheepishly called the police.

Naturally, he was unable to tell them where he was (it turned out to be about 1.5 kilometres from the spot he'd been found days before). But luckily, the police were able to track him through his phone – and so only waste about four hours on another chopper.

'In my own personal experience this hasn't happened before,' said a less-than-impressed Senior Sergeant Michael Potts.

> It's disappointing after speaking to him last week and stressing our concerns that he'd gone out and got lost, that he's gone out to the same area and got lost again. We're hoping to find out from him why he's gone right back out there again ... We're experiencing a hot, dry climate and this guy was fortunate the weather had cooled down again. People with limited supplies don't tend to last very long in this sort of climate. Without his mobile phone it would have been a stab in the dark to find him.

I wish no ill of any man. But a stab in the dark might be just what Mr Lake needed.

A Snowball's Chance

Aussies who survived being lost in the snow

'Luck, like a Russian car, generally only
works if you push it.'
Tom Holt, British novelist

Want some fun facts about Mount Everest?

Well, good news: I can give you four.

Fact number one: it's not the world's tallest mountain. Technically speaking, that title goes to Mauna Kea, a Hawaiian island that's really an underwater volcano, one mostly submerged by the sea.

Fact number two: you pronounce it all wrong. It's not actually 'EVER-rest', as nice as that sounds. The name is not some vaguely poetic reference to the mountain's eternal tranquillity or majestic state of repose. It's a nod to a British surveyor called George. Whose surname was always pronounced 'EVE-rest'.

Now for fact number three ... which is not quite as fun. In fact, it's a teensy bit grim. Mount Everest is not just home to icy cliffs and jagged rocks and unstable ridges and clobbering winds. It is not just home to landslides and avalanches and below-freezing temperatures, next to no oxygen and the occasional bear. It is also home to more than 200 dead bodies. Climbers who set out to conquer the mountain but were never quite able to make it back down, their bodies are tucked into crevices, buried under ridges and beneath icy cliffs. In all probability they will never be found, let alone taken home for a funeral.

Australian members of this grisly club include a Melbourne medical student named Craig Nottle and a Queensland scientist called Fred From. Both amateur climbers lost their footing on a ledge back in 1984 and disappeared into a gully below. On a more positive note, that year also saw fifty-two-year-old Mike Rheinberger become the oldest ever Australian to make it all the way to the top. On a less positive note, he is still there to this day, after showing 'signs of exhaustion, dehydration, cerebral oedema, retinal haemorrhages and possible blood clots in his upper legs'.

In the decades since then, Nottle, From and Rheinberger have been joined by Adelaide's Mark Auricht (who 'may have suffered a heart attack or stroke') and Queensland's Francesco Enrico Marchetti, who fell to altitude sickness.

(Altitude sickness, in case you're wondering, is a sort of present that awaits climbers if they can get 8000 metres above sea level – a part of the mountain that's attractively known as the death zone. Essentially the result of an extreme lack of oxygen, which crushes the lungs and swells up your brain, fun side effects include psychosis, blindness, dizziness, paralysis, bowel disfunction and a leaky bladder. Not to mention nausea, fatigue, shortness of breath and a cough so strong that it can crack your ribs, cause internal bleeding, and see you choke to death on your blood.)

All of which is by way of bringing us to fact number four: human bodies work best at ground level. Climbing Mount Everest is a pastime for maniacs. Maniacs much like Lincoln Hall.

Born and raised in Canberra – a fact that may well help explain why he had no fear of death – fifty-one-year-old Hall became the latest Australian to be left for dead back in May 2006 when he collapsed at an altitude of 8700 metres. His two exhausted Sherpa guides tried to revive him for more than two hours, despite the fact that darkness was falling, their oxygen tanks were low, and Hall himself was not just unconscious and unable to move, but also shitting his pants. With several guides having already perished that season, the expedition's leaders were not keen to lose even more. So they eventually radioed the pair to abandon Hall's body and do what they could to survive.

Happily, the Sherpas managed to make it to safety. Hall's family was informed of his death later that night, and the news quickly made its way into the morning papers.

So it's safe to say that an English climber named Myles Osborne may have been just a teensy bit surprised by the sight that awaited him the next afternoon, which he later wrote about in his memoir.

Sitting to our left, about two feet from a 10,000-foot drop, was a man. Not dead, not sleeping, but sitting cross legged, in the process of changing his shirt. He had his down suit unzipped to the waist, his arms out of the sleeves, was wearing no hat, no gloves, no sunglasses, had no oxygen mask, regulator, ice axe, oxygen, no sleeping bag, no mattress, no food nor water bottle. 'I imagine you're surprised to see me here', he said. Now, this was a moment of total disbelief to us all. Here was a gentleman, apparently lucid, who had spent the night without oxygen at 8600m, without proper equipment and barely clothed.

Freezing, dehydrated and slightly delirious, Hall had lost eight fingers to frostbite, along with a toe, and for some reason decided to shed some of his clothes. But he had managed to hang on to the most important thing – luck. It's still a bit of a mystery how on earth he survived.

'It was a case of me rejecting death and insisting on life,' was the way the climber himself explained it, not long before dying of cancer in 2012.

I wasn't going to let it happen, I just had to stay alive, and somehow stay awake till the morning when at least there would be some sun, which would carry some sort of warmth ... My Christian and Muslim friends call it a miracle, my climbing friends say I am a lucky bastard, and my Buddhist friends say I must have more to do on this Earth.

Gilian Lee also has more to do on this Earth. And I suspect that a lot of it is going to be pretty stupid. A young public servant from (yes) Canberra, one of his life goals is to climb the world's eight tallest mountains ... without the use of an oxygen tank.

Breathing, after all, would be cheating. '[If I used a tank], I might as well chop 50 per cent of the mountain height off,' is how this intrepid bureaucrat explains his bold quest. 'I will never take supplemental oxygen, as it is just not me ... Defeats the purpose of being there in the first place, in my opinion.'

If you wish to hear some of Lee's other thoughts, you can check out his blog or his tweets or his Facebook or his Instagram. Or you can just hit yourself in the head with a brick, as that will be about as fun and save a great deal of time. Either way, the general gist is that he tried to climb Everest in this way in 2015, 2017 and 2018, and, predictably enough, completely failed every time. Not because the idea was a dumb one, mind you, but because he kept being 'horrendously let down by the expedition company'.

So the year 2019 saw Lee make his way back to the mountain with a brand-new plan in mind. No, he wasn't going to use an oxygen tank, please don't be silly. This time, he was going to do the climb solo.

'This will be the last throw of the dice,' our hero blogged from base camp. 'I am running out of [money] to keep chasing this dream.' The problem was he would be throwing these dice with a chest infection and a 'killer sore throat' and doing so in dreadful weather conditions that had recently killed several climbers. 'Plans getting worse by the day. Lot of wind at the summit from the south side direction,' he wrote on Facebook. 'North side windy as well. Every day of delay is a nightmare.'

But do such things really matter when you have courage and pluck, guts and grit? Nerves of steel, a will of iron, and a heart that seems to be made from sheer balls?

Well, yes. I'm afraid that they do. Lee collapsed within a couple of days – unconscious, cold, sick and alone (unless you count the lungs full of blood). And with nobody else crazy enough to climb in that weather, that really should have been the end of our story (and, in better news, the end of his blog).

Lady Luck, however, can come in all sorts of forms. In this case, she came as two alpine workers who had decided to take advantage of the lull in climbing to try to carry out a few minor repairs. Somehow they stumbled across Lee's body. And while no doubt feeling tempted to just stumble on, they eventually managed to attach him to their yak and drag him down to safety.

'[It was] the most uncomfortable ride known to mankind,' our dauntless hero wrote many weeks later, when he was out of intensive care. 'It was just pure agony and pain, but I didn't care.'

'Pure agony and pain' are not only treats that await climbers on Everest. They can also be found at the South Pole. Long before Edmund Hillary and Tenzing Norgay, fans of hypothermia, frostbite, trench foot and needless suffering tended to spend their time in Antarctica. Sure, it was a huge frozen wasteland, thousands of kilometres from anywhere. Sure, it was covered in glaciers, crevasses, earthquakes, volcanoes and ice sheets that could crack up in seconds. Sure, it was prone to sub-zero temperatures and rib-breaking winds, blinding blizzards and murderous storms. The point was that, back then, no one had ever really mapped it. Helping to do so would make you immortal. Even if, in the process, you died.

Such, at least, was the thinking of the future Sir, Douglas Mawson, an 'earnest and determined' graduate of the University of Adelaide, where he later lectured in mineralogical science. Having 'won distinction' as part of a 1909 English expedition to Antarctica ('winning distinction' being code for 'not dying'), the tall, skinny twenty-five-year-old decided it was time for Australia to do some exploring of its own. The country's honour seemed to demand it. And its mining and whaling industries could be quite well served, too.

So, after raising millions from assorted commercial quarters, Mawson's Australasian Antarctic Expedition set off from Hobart in December 1910. After surviving a series of huge waves that 'repeatedly [threatened to] overwhelm the ship', they arrived six weeks later in what we now know to be the world's windiest place: a rocky inlet surrounded by high ice cliffs, where they set up camp and built a small hut. Mawson, who was responsible for team morale, described the conditions as 'grisly, fierce and appalling'. 'This world is a void,' that cheery optimist wrote in his diary. 'We stumble and struggle through the Stygian gloom; the merciless blast – an incubus of vengeance – stabs, buffets and freezes; the stinging drift blinds and chokes.'

Unless you have ever been to, say, Crown Casino, it's probably hard to think of a worse place. But Mawson was apparently determined to find one, so launched a plan to take the venture inland. Splitting his team into four small groups, in order to better explore the surrounding ice, he chose the longest and hardest expedition himself: a 1500-kilometre-round-trek through a blizzard-prone area. A blizzard-prone area that was pitted with incredibly deep crevasses, most of them hidden under a thin lid of snow.

With two companions, three sleds, sixteen huskies and 800 kilograms of supplies, he duly set off for five disaster-free weeks. But it was a bit much to hope that there could be a sixth. Catastrophe finally came when the three were still about 500 kilometres away from the safe Stygian gloom of the hut. One moment, Lieutenant Belgrave Ninnis, a twenty-three-year-old British army officer, was right there beside them – or at least dimly visible in the endless grey mist. Then the next moment, he, his sled and his six huskies were gone. In their place lay a black 'yawning chasm' about 10 feet wide and 100 feet deep. A chasm in which, if you listened very carefully, you could just hear the whine of a dog.

'For three hours we called unceasingly but no answering sound came back,' wrote Mawson, later that night. 'The dog had ceased to moan. A chill draught was blowing out of the abyss. We felt that there was little hope.'

While the death of a colleague is always sad (unless you happen to work in one of the four major banks), this loss was a particularly big problem for Mawson because it also came with a loss of supplies. Ninnis's lost sled had been carrying 'practically all the food', along with essential items like spades, picks and tents.

Mawson and his remaining companion – Xavier Mertz, a twenty-eight-year-old Swiss lawyer – had maybe a week's worth of meals, if they rationed them very carefully. And they were at least four weeks' march from the hut.

Still, chin up. Stiff upper lip. What doesn't kill you, mustn't grumble, etc. Over the following days, our doughty heroes slowly made their way through the little food that remained – and, apparently, a whole lot of their skin. 'The sight of my feet gave me quite a shock,' the 'exhausted, weak and chilled' Mawson wrote of the day that he took off his boots – and discovered they were attached to his soles. 'Abundant watery fluid had escaped into the socks,' he says in the course of a charming passage about weeping blisters.

Mind you, things weren't going that much better around his 'nose and lips' – both of which had 'broken open'. And I feel it's important for you to know that his groin was also 'getting in a painfully raw condition due to reduced condition, dampness and friction in walking.'

Still, at least the pair had food during those first few days. After that, they had to snack on the huskies. 'George, the poorest of the dogs, was killed and partly fed to the others, partly kept for ourselves,' wrote Mawson about this organic repast. 'The meat was roughly fried on the lid of the aluminium cooker, an operation which resulted in little more than scorching the surface. On the whole, it was voted good though it had a strong, musty taste and was so stringy that it could not be properly chewed.'

Minutes later, however, this budding food critic started to notice a few minor issues beyond the fibrous mouthfeel. Crippling nausea was one. Thunderous diarrhea was another. Hair loss, exhaustion, violent seizures and insanity all seemed to feature in among the third. Dog livers, you see, contain toxically high levels of vitamin A, which can bring on a deadly condition called hypervitaminosis.

Two weeks of dog meals later, Xavier Mertz duly succumbed. 'During the afternoon he has several fits and is delirious, fills his trousers again and I clean out for him,' the ever-detail-oriented Mawson noted in that day's diary.

> He is very weak, becomes more and more delirious, rarely being able to speak coherently. At 8pm he raves and breaks a tent pole. I hold him down, then he becomes more peaceful and I put him quietly in the bag. He dies peacefully at about 2am on the morning of the 8th. He had lost all the skin of his legs and private parts.

And, just in case you were wondering, Mawson himself was in the 'same condition. My whole body is apparently rotting from want of proper nourishment – frost-bitten fingertips, festerings, mucous membrane of nose gone, saliva glands of mouth refusing duty, skin coming off the whole body.'

By this stage, our dog-eating diarist had been due back at camp for well over two weeks and still had 160 kilometres to go. He was barely able to stand on his two blistered feet. How on earth was he going to trudge back while eating food that simply made him more ill?

The answer, of course, was with luck. While there can be no doubt that Mawson had some truly heroic levels of determination and endurance – this was, after all, a man who had spent years in Adelaide – such qualities would not have been nearly enough were it not for a huge slice of luck in the form of a man named Frank Hurley. The official photographer for the Australasian Expedition, Hurley had been part of a party that had set out from base camp to find the three missing explorers when they had failed to return a fortnight before. They didn't manage to find them, of course, but at the last moment Hurley decided to leave behind a small bag of food, on the vanishingly small chance that Mawson might see it.

He did. As Hurley himself wrote, many years later, 'a miracle happened through the blinding snowdrift'. With endless stretches of flat, white ice in every direction, and a thick, white mist making it impossible to see more than a few feet in front, the emaciated explorer 'ran practically straight into a mound, with a black speck on the top of it. Taking this speck down, he found that it was a bag of food that had been left by Hodgman, McLean and I, who had been sent out to search for the overdue party.'

Fortified by actual food, Mawson was able to make it back to camp a little over a week later.

A few years after that he was, alas, back in Adelaide. All good luck tends to run out eventually.

All at Sea

Aussies who survived being lost in the ocean

'Success is simply a matter of luck. Ask any failure.'

Earl Wilson, US columnist

Priced at a cool $200k, the LeisureCat Sportsfisher is a 'high-speed catamaran capable of delivering a comfortable and stable ride in adverse weather conditions'. Or at least, that's what they say in the ad.

Stephen Knight, however, may well have said something different after a less than 'comfortable and stable' fishing trip in 2014. After anchoring said catamaran in Serrurier Island, about 50 kilometres off the WA coast, he and a few friends had enjoyed a pleasant day's fishing and were all set for a pleasant night's sleep.

The weather, however, had other ideas. Ideas that you might call 'adverse'.

'A big storm came in,' the veteran Perth sailor later recalled, 'one of those super-cell storms [with] 40-knot winds and gusts at 60-knots.' The winds were so strong, in fact, they ripped Knight's 8-metre boat from the dock and dragged it several miles out to sea. 'We could still see it because it had its anchor light on. We watched it through the course of the whole night.'

It was well into the next day by the time help arrived, and by that time Knight's precious vessel was well out of view. And that's how it stayed over the following days, as planes systematically searched through the area, finding nary a trace. In due course, the catamaran was declared sunk, Knight cursed his luck and the Earth continued to spin.

Eight months later, however, something rather strange happened, a little over 7400 kilometres from where the boat was last seen. Yes, you guessed it. It was seen again. Washed up on a small island on the east coast of Africa.

'I basically thought it would be on the bottom of the ocean somewhere,' said the stunned fisherman after being reunited with his baby, 'but it floated across the Indian Ocean without anyone seeing it or spotting it ... To find it after all of this time is just unbelievable.'

It's a story that seems even more unbelievable when you think about all the international shipping lanes that crisscross those waters. One of the world's busiest maritime routes (because it connects Asia with Europe), the Indian Ocean sees more than 20,000 merchant ships a year, crisscrossing its shipping lanes like 20,000 strands of spaghetti. How could absolutely none of them – not even one single, measly ship – have spotted Knight's 8-metre-long boat?

Well, quite easily, as it happens.

Planet Earth, it turns out, is a very big place, and salt water covers about 70 per cent of it. The reason why pirates and 'people smugglers' are so hard to catch, and illegal fishing boats are so enormously common, is that such law-breakers have 361 million square kilometres to hide in. They can do all their law-breaking almost completely unseen. If you happen to be considering a career change one day, they are all options that deserve careful thought.

But if you happen to be considering going missing one day, I really hope that you're not in the ocean. Chances are, you'll be quite hard to find.

Think about Malaysia Airlines Flight 370, for example: a 60-metre-long plane with 60-metre-wide wings, and thousands of big floaty items aboard. And think about the way that all 100 tonnes of it just disappeared, way back in 2014.

'The simple reality is that even today, [planes and] ships go missing all the time without a trace,' says Jim Delgado, NOAA's director of maritime heritage. UNESCO estimates that around three million shipwrecks currently litter the ocean floor, and it's a safe bet that plenty of them spent days, months or years much like Knight's catamaran, drifting unnoticed through the vast, endless seas. Until they were finally sunk by a steady build-up of rainwater. Or toppled by a wind, wave or reef.

An interesting thought, I think you'll agree, but not everyone would find it a comforting one. Ben Tooki, for instance, may have preferred not to dwell on such matters during a fishing-trip-gone-wrong in 2005. A twenty-two-year-old butcher from Tennant Creek, Tooki's idea of fun was to fly to the Pacific, get in a boat, cast a rod and see what he could catch. But his hobby became a lot less fun the day that he, his mate and his uncle took their little tin boat to Kiribati, a group of tiny islands 5500 kilometres north of New Zealand. While travelling from one tiny island to another – a trip of about 40 kilometres – the three suddenly found themselves battling a tropical storm for hours on end and being thrown ever more wildly off course.

Which would have been fine once the winds, waves and rips had subsided. Were it not for the fact that they had completely run out of petrol. Stuck in a 12-foot tinnie with two litres of water, a bunch of bananas and nothing in the way of a phone, flare or radio, they were forced to simply drift through the day, and throughout the night, in the hope of spotting a boat or perhaps hitting dry land.

Six weeks later, this was still the plan. But it still hadn't quite come off. Despite countless searches, their little boat remained an imperceptible grey speck in an infinitely vast swathe of blue. Dehydrated, emaciated, sunburnt, sunstruck and pursued by the odd tiger shark, the three lived on fish, birds and turtles, which they caught using their own skin as bait. Or they just ate some of the green algae that had built up on the boat.

With conversation beginning to pall after the first week or four, they essentially passed the time waiting for rain to fall into their mouths. But by day forty-five, they were essentially waiting to die.

'I reckon[ed] he wasn't going to make the next day,' said Ben of his diabetic, forty-seven-year-old uncle, who was the worst hit of the three. 'I was just slowly dying too.' Now more than 500 kilometres south of Kiribati, he decided that the only option was to 'just finish myself off if I'm still alive' in two days and his uncle, who needed him, was not.

But, as luck would have it, no such plan was required – and it was all thanks to one Cyclone Olaf. A Category 5 cyclone with an extra-cool name, Olaf had spent the previous day ravaging a path through the southern Pacific Ocean, a few thousand kilometres north of New Zealand. Worried about people in places like Samoa, New Zealand's Air Force dispatched a fleet to patrol the region and see what they might be able to find in the way of survivors. What they ended up finding, of course, was a tiny tin fishing boat. All three fishermen frail and thin. But alive.

Not a perfect holiday, in retrospect, but it probably still beats forty-five days in Nimbin. And at least they were in a boat that whole time. Not a big one, sure, with a roof and a telly. But even a little boat is better than treading water.

Such would, in any event, have been the view of a certain Ross Chapman if you had asked him on 3 January 2017. A thirty-year-old boilermaker and keen amateur fisherman, he had begun the day about 50 kilometres from the WA coast, trawling for marlin in his small motorboat. This involved having the boat's engine on, so it could move with, tire out and eventually pull in the (huge) fish, once they became ensnared in the net.

It did not, in theory, involve him accidentally falling off his boat and then watching it motor away.

But in practice, this is exactly what happened. Wearing nothing but shorts – i.e. no life jacket – Chapman suddenly found himself floating in shark-infested waters, completely alone and 50 kilometres away from the shore.

How long can a fit person survive treading water, under a hot, beating sun, while being battered by big endless waves? The answer, in my case, would be roughly ten minutes, give or take nine minutes and fifty-five seconds. Chapman, however, was still more or less alive after six lonely hours – which gave his guardian angel just enough time.

Said angel took the form of a 250 kilogram marlin, which had been ensnared by another boat several kilometres away. Apparently not super keen to be caught, it fought the good fight, taking 700 metres of line, forcing the crew to veer wildly off course. And then it somehow managed to snap off the line 'at just the right time' to allow one crew member to briefly glimpse something odd. Was that a little boat in the grey waves beyond? Or, more to the point, a little boat with nobody inside it?

After motoring over to investigate, and discovering that the answer was yes, the crew alerted the maritime authorities, who quickly organised a search. An 'absolutely rooted' Chapman was eventually located, still afloat and shark-free – but by this point slightly less keen on fishing.

'It was probably the best feeling I have ever had in my life seeing that boat coming towards me,' he told the media after being discharged from hospital, where he had had to overcome hypothermia. 'I consider myself very lucky. I know how much of a big deal it was that I did get found. I know how big that ocean is out there.'

John Quinn probably has a pretty good idea too these days, after having a similar time in the torrid Bass Strait. The forty-nine-year-old skipper of the 35-foot yacht *MEM*, he shot to fame during the 1993 Sydney to Hobart – a notoriously dangerous yacht race that has killed six sailors to date and destroyed countless dozens of boats.

The thing about this strait, as all sailors know, is that it's not actually a sane place to sail in. The main reason being that it's extremely shallow, and therefore extremely susceptible to strong winds and waves. Strong winds, waves and currents that come through all the time, because the strait is right in the path of the 'Roaring Forties'. These are the wild westerly winds that rip right around the Southern Ocean, unimpeded by land, until they're forced to funnel their way in between Vic and Tassie.

That's why this notorious stretch of water is now home to at least 1000 shipwrecks and many, many more dead sailors. And why John Quinn was all set to join them, when a 23-foot-high wave momentarily knocked the *MEM* sideways during a violent storm at 11.30pm.

'It came from an odd direction,' he later recalled. 'Picked us up, threw us straight over on her side. We had three down below, fortunately. All of us on deck, I think bar one, went over the side.'

Fortunately for his crew, they were all wearing safety harnesses, and soon managed to climb back on board.

Unfortunately for John, his harness snapped, leaving him bobbing all in the cold, storm-whipped waters. Battered by 20-foot waves. Deafened by 150 kilometre winds. Completely alone. And completely shrouded in darkness.

'The chances of seeing one individual off a yacht in those sorts of conditions in the middle of the night are sweet fuck-all,' said the veteran sailor and wordsmith, who somehow managed to stay conscious and afloat for the next five hours, despite starting to get hypothermia.

The chances of *hearing* one individual off a yacht in those sorts of conditions, on other hand, turned to out to be slightly better.

'I was on the wing of the bridge, portside lookout, wearing my raincoat and rain hat when I thought I heard a scream,' says Bernie Holmes, a seaman aboard a 100,000-tonne oil tanker that just happened to be passing through. 'With all the wind and rain, I wasn't sure, so I took off my hat, and then I positively heard the scream. I directed my searchlight toward the area – and there he was, waving and screaming.'

But while Quinn was only about 20 metres away, that turned out to be 20 metres too far. 'The scary part was we spotted him, and then he drifted out of the searchlight, and then he was in the dark again.'

Unable to find the yachtsman, the tanker sent out a call for help. It was quickly received on the *Atara* – a 40-foot yacht that had also entered that year's Sydney to Hobart and been forced to give up in the face of fierce waves. 'We were on our way home [but we] went back to help look for him and nearly ran over him,' recalled a crewmember. 'He saw us – we didn't see him. He had no light; there were no strobes and personal EPIRBs in those days. He was just a dark blob in the grey ocean.' A dark blob that they just happened to sail within two or three feet of, during a rare moment in which the waves had subsided.

The AHS *Centaur*, on the other hand, was 'ablaze with lights' when it was torpedoed by a Japanese submarine back in 1943. Also covered in bright red crosses, the Australian hospital ship was supposed to be immune to attack under international law, when it set sail from Sydney to PNG carrying hundreds of medicos. But that didn't stop it from being struck without warning at 4.10am, in what then-PM John Curtin described as a 'deliberate, wanton and barbarous attack'.

By 4.13am, *Centaur* was at the bottom of the ocean, along with the bulk of its 332 passengers. With almost everyone on board having been asleep below deck, survival for the few who weren't killed straightaway was a matter of scrambling upstairs, through a maze of narrow, smoky corridors. And then hoping that when the ship went down in a flaming whirlpool of metal, the associated suction wouldn't drag them down too.

The good news was that around a hundred passengers managed to make it to 4.15.

The bad news was that they found themselves afloat in the middle of the ocean, and without any way to communicate. Australia was 80 kilometres to the west. And no one actually knew where they were.

The day accordingly saw the number of survivors begin to shrink, as exhausted passengers succumbed to burns and shrapnel wounds, or fell prey to the ever-circling sharks. 'It was a worry all right,' remembers Dick Medcalf. 'The sharks were there as far down as you could see and they never left us.'

By day two, the numbers were down to just sixty-four. Sixty-four survivors who were becoming ever more scattered over huge swathes of ocean, and as such, ever harder to see. Sixty-four survivors with no food or water – and one would presume not all that much sleep. They were trapped in a world of fear, pain and suffering. A world unlike any I myself have endured, unless you count that time my parents took me to *Riverdance*.

I think it's fair to say that these folks were due a stroke of luck.

And I think it's fair to say that one duly arrived.

While WWII had made merchant ships a rare sight in the Pacific, it had made RAAF flights a great deal more common. The *Centaur* just happened to have gone down in the general region of Bundaberg, where 300 young pilots had been posted to a small training school and from which they were dispatched on the occasional mission.

When a small convoy of US ships was due to pass through the area, twenty-year-old Jack Keith was sent out to escort it, for a learning exercise as much as anything else. Being a young, risk-taking type who still had a great deal to learn, he spent a fair bit of that trip flying at a stupidly low height – a stupidly low height that gave him a great view of the sea.

> We were patrolling mainly from the front but at the end of our time on sortie so we came around the back to do an antisubmarine sweep. As we then turned back towards the convoy, we saw a discoloration in the water well to the south, so we turned back for a look.

He saw a single little lifeboat, with one word painted on it – that word, of course, being *Centaur*.

> As soon as we saw it was the *Centaur*, a hospital ship, we thought 'well, flaming Charlie, things are a bit rough – they shouldn't do such things.' ... If we hadn't have seen them I don't think there would have been a future for them because the convoy had gone out, and there wouldn't have been any other ships around there for seven days.

Cripes! Flaming Charlie indeed!

No Chance in Hell

Aussies who survived natural disasters

'Every day a piano doesn't fall on my head is good luck.'

Meg Rosoff, US writer

Have you ever had a bit of a sinking feeling?

Three people from Moree know just how you feel. Two men and a woman, who wish to remain nameless, were standing by the swollen banks of the Mehi River during NSW's 2021 floods, watching all the water-sodden chaos unfold. All in all, it was a pretty good night, insofar as nights in Moree go.

But then, all of a sudden, the ground gave way beneath them. I don't mean this metaphorically. I mean this quite literally. They found themselves at the bottom of a sinkhole. A gigantic sinkhole that, with so much rain flooding into it, would shortly become a watery tomb.

Do I exaggerate? No, I do not. Moree is not exactly a bustling metropolis at the best of times, but at this particular moment, it was pelting with rain, and just before midnight, and every street had long since been evacuated. The nearest house was a long way away; the nearest resident perhaps further still. Barely able to be heard over the deafening rain, the three people kept on screaming for help, but they certainly didn't expect to receive it.

Some kind of miracle would clearly be required if they were to make it to the next day. And wouldn't you know it, a miracle arrived. It came in the form of a little fire alarm at a little hospital a little way down the road, which suddenly decided to make a noise for no reason. Within a short time, a fire truck drove by, complete with ladders and ropes – and a firefighter with exceptionally good hearing.

Rescued, as they were, in just a few hours and in near-perfect shape, the 'Moree Three' never got as much media as their dramatic predicament probably deserved. For a natural disaster to really dominate the headlines, you see – for a flood, quake or fire to really own the front page – the media needs to see at least one gruesome injury. Or, better still, a long, gruesome death. And in an ideal world, of course, the victim's suffering would be captured on film and they would not keep their name a big secret.

But the best possible scenario for a hardworking editor in need of a headline is having a victim who has a name you can rhyme. Folks, I give you Stuart Diver. The 'Thredbo Survivor'.

A twenty-seven-year-old ski instructor with perfect cheekbones, straight white teeth and immaculate hair, Diver was fast asleep around midnight back in July 1997 after a long, hard day of teaching uncos to snowplough. Suddenly, a 'rumbling' sound rang out through the small alpine village – a deafening shriek some compared to 'a freight train'. It was the sound of 3500 tonnes of rock, mud and concrete careering down the mountain and crashing into two ski lodges. Completely crushing and covering them both. And burying the nineteen people inside.

Arriving on the scene a little after midnight, Thredbo's search-and-rescue team was not just faced with a 2000-cubic-metre mound of snow-covered debris. It was faced with a pitch-black night and a bleak, all-encompassing silence.

Hopes were low that they would actually find any survivors. And those hopes only got lower over the following two days. Battling heavy snow and subzero temperatures as they extracted steel beams, the one hundred searchers only managed to find four very dead bodies in among chunks of concrete and rock. By day three, the 'rescue' was officially relabelled. It was now just a grim search for human remains.

Then, sixty-five long hours after the landslide first hit, a muffled sound faintly emerged from the pile. 'Can anyone hear me?' a rescue worker called out in response.

'I can hear you,' Stuart Diver replied.

Miraculously unscathed apart from a bad case of frostbite, Diver had somehow ended up under a huge concrete slab. A concrete slab that had been angled in just such a way that it (a) didn't crush him and (b) stopped him from being crushed by the vast weight above. And best of all, (c) it created a tiny pocket of air that allowed him to breathe – not just a bit, but for almost four days. It was cold, it was damp. It was cramped and pitch black. But, as luck would have it, it had kept him alive.

'It was hell. I am scared of the dark and I'm claustrophobic,' Diver later said of his time in this underground coffin. 'I could hear the work going on above me and I knew they were searching for people. They had to be. I could hear the machinery, the choppers. Even conversations.'

'No matter how much I shouted or what noise I made, I couldn't make them hear me [until the time at last came that they did]. I didn't pick myself out to survive, it just happened. It was fate.'

But how lucky was this guy *really*? Yes, eighteen other people died in that landslide, and he miraculously managed not to be one of them. But those eighteen victims weren't just nodding acquaintances. They included his wife, who he saw and heard die. If Diver's survival was indeed 'fate', it sounds a bit to me like a fate worse than death – or, at the very least, a fate that wasn't all that much better.

When you think about it, wouldn't he actually have been luckier if there was no landslide in the first place? If 30 July 1997 had just been a perfectly ordinary, humdrum, dull kind of day? A day not worth writing about? A day not worth remembering? A day that was, in short, kind of blah?

It's a thought that's worth pondering, right here and now, if you yourself are having an ordinary day too. A day that's full of long, pointless tasks, or long, pointless tiffs with your nearest and dearest. Maybe you have a sore throat, or you can't find your keys, or you're

That the First Fleet made it to Australia at all, let alone before the French did, was just the beginning of their luck.

'A vixen and a terrible liar and the most artful and profane woman that ever lived.' Eliza Fraser of Fraser Island fame managed to survive a shipwreck. But those who were forced to spend time with her didn't feel quite so lucky.

The 'wild white man' of Wye River. Escaped convict William Buckley had Buckley's chance of surviving the outback – that is, until he was adopted by the Wathaurong people ...

Lost, alone and dying in the rainforest after a terrible plane crash? Then hope there's someone like Bernard O'Reilly out there willing to hike 40 kilometres on a hunch he might find you.

Lucky new owners of the Welcome Stranger: the biggest gold nugget that you'll ever see. Or, in fact, that anyone has ever seen.

RC Packer, James's great-grandfather, started the family's fortune, but could he have done it without the ten-shilling coin he found on the ground at a Tasmanian racecourse?

Clontarf, New South Wales: the attempted assassination of Prince Alfred, budding alcoholic and bona fide pants man. That the prince didn't die and set off a wave of violence through the colony is nothing short of a miracle.

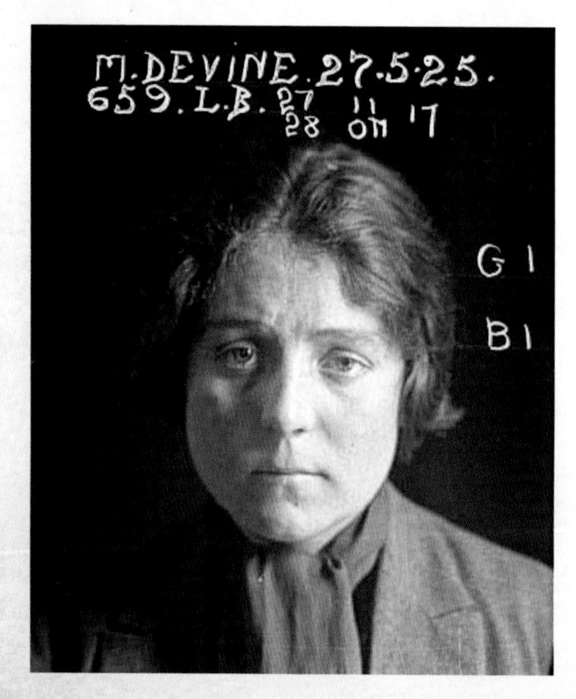

Tilly Devine, savvy sex worker turned entrepreneurial brothel madam, only managed to keep out of jail thanks to a handy loophole ...

Shirley Beiger was blessed with the kinds of looks and charm that the media adore – which is handy when you're trying to get away with murder. (Mitchell Library, State Library of New South Wales)

Errol Flynn, an actor who never really had to act. Which was fortunate, given he couldn't.

Snowy Baker: possibly Australia's finest ever sportsman.
But not, perhaps, our most sporting.

Speedskater Steve Bradbury. Doing a Bradbury. (Getty Images)

When is a lake not just a lake? When it's Lake Toba, a massive volcano – one that's possibly the reason *Homo sapiens* are the only humans around.

The imaginatively named Eastern Brown Snake – a snake from the east which is brown – is one of Australia's deadliest creatures. But one lucky two-year-old boy managed to survive being bitten twice by one of these highly venomous reptiles.

The world's second-tallest mountain, Mount Everest (which, by the way, you've been pronouncing all wrong), is, horrifically, littered with corpses. But Lincoln Hall is not one of them.

Stuart Diver, Thredbo landslide survivor, owes his life to a concrete slab. (Above left: AAP Image)

Olaf, a Category 5 cyclone with a super cool name, might look dangerous,
but three lost fishermen owe their lives to it.

waiting for a call back from 'customer service'. Or maybe it's late and you're tired but you have to stay up, because you're behind on a book and a draft is due soon.

The point is that however blerg your day may have been, it has not featured some kind of natural disaster. And this, my friend, makes you much, much luckier than the Stuart Divers of this world – much, much luckier than all the people who somehow found themselves facing death, even if they managed to escape it unscathed. The truly lucky people are the ones who have never had to dodge a cyclone, outrun a tsunami, flee a fire or stay afloat in a flood.

The truly lucky people, in short, are the people like us. Because planet Earth can be pretty lethal. For all that we should appreciate the majesty of nature – its forests, its flowers, its mountains, its lakes – we should also take a moment to appreciate the fact that all of that outdoors shit can kill you. Every new year doesn't just bring forth a new batch of babies: innocent little souls with love in their hearts and poo on their plump, rosy bottoms. It brings forth a new batch of heatwaves and a new batch of cold snaps and a new batch of droughts, storms and earthquakes.

And, with climate change creating ever more extreme weather, and sea levels continuing to rise, it's likely that the years to come will bring even more natural catastrophes. The UN's Office for Disaster Risk Reduction recently predicted that they'll jump from an average of 400 a year in 2015 to 560 by 2030. That's a 40 per cent increase. And after that, God only knows. There will come a time when these new babies get old and look back on the world as it is right now. 'Those guys had it good,' these now far less innocent and rosy-cheeked souls will say. 'They were very lucky to live when they did.'

And there's no doubt they'll be right.

It's also worth noting that, even if we manage to get a hold of global warming, acts of God can still strike from above. We're generally pretty upbeat when it comes to the solar system – all those lovely little specks that light up our night sky. Byron called them 'the poetry of heaven'; Wordsworth called them 'the spirits of the blessed'. But both of those bards would have been a whole lot less lyrical if they were pumping out their poems a few billion years earlier. This seemingly sedate little slice of the galaxy was like a big game of dodgem cars, with huge asteroids and comets coming from every direction, and crashing into Earth with catastrophic results. We can't see most of the damage now, because of the way tectonic plates shift and reshape the Earth's surface, but we only have to look at all those craters on the moon to get an idea of how often this kind of thing happened.

But here's the thing. They're still happening. It was only sixty-six million years ago that a massive asteroid mostly wiped out the dinosaurs. Probably more than 10 kilometres wide, it was travelling at something like 60,000 kilometres per hour when it struck with the force of five billion nuclear bombs.

And it was only about a 110 years ago that something similar seems to have happened in Siberia, albeit on a much smaller scale. Not so much a tourist hotspot as a place where people are sent as a punishment, this sparsely populated stretch of Russia lost around 80 million trees in the blink of an eye when an incoming meteor exploded before hitting the ground.

And it was only in 2013 that a 12,000-tonne meteor entered the Earth's atmosphere completely undetected by scientists, only to burst 30 kilometres above the ground. Taking place in the remote Southern Urals, the blast was still equivalent in force to more than thirty Hiroshimas and managed to damage 7200 buildings, seriously injuring many of the people inside.

Plenty of flying rocks have continued to hit the planet since then. In fact, plenty of have hit the planet since I started typing this sentence. And more have arrived since I finished it. Visitors from outer space are actually rather commonplace: astronomers estimate that that something like 100,000 kilograms of cosmic debris enters the Earth's atmosphere each day. Sometimes in the mildly dangerous form of a meteorite. But more often in the form of a pebble so small that it quickly vaporises into fine dust.

Still, there's nothing to say that a big rock's not out there, completely unknown to science and coming straight for Cowra or Cairns.

We're pretty sure that the planet had a near miss back in 1883, when a fragmented comet as big as the one that wiped out the dinosaurs seemed to get within a few hundred kilometres. A blurry smudge in a primitive photograph, and still a source of astronomical dispute to this day, the 'Bonilla comet' – if it actually existed – would have likely weighed about a billion tonnes.

Either way, as the B612 Foundation puts it, 'It's 100 percent certain we'll be hit by a devastating asteroid' – the only real question is when. A big one could hit anywhere, any time. So any day it does not is a good one.

And then there's the fact that the sun – which we all know is going to expand and kill us one day – sometimes looks like it's trying to get ahead of schedule. What humans never quite realised in the days before electricity is that the sun occasionally emits 'solar flares'. Completely invisible to your average cave dweller, according to researcher Matthew Blackett these 'intense clouds of energetic photons and particles' can have 'the energy of millions of hydrogen bombs exploding at once'. Littlish flares shoot out from the sun pretty much all the time, float invisibly through space for however many days, and generally miss Earth by millions of miles. When they do hit, they might cause a few blackouts, disrupt a few flights and maybe mess with your modem. Chances are, you've experienced one without even realising it. A little flare is not a big deal.

But the day will soon come when a huge one hits, just like in 1859. In today's wired-up society, a solar flare of the scale of the Carrington Event would not just wipe out a handful of telegraph lines (the only electrical infrastructure around at the time). It could bring down the internet, radio and GPS. It could cause blackouts all over the world. Trillions of dollars could fall from the stock market. Planes and satellites could well fall from the sky.

According to the University of Colorado's Daniel Baker, the Earth came very close to being hit by just such a flare back in 2012. 'In my view, the July 2012 solar storm was in all respects at least as strong as the 1859 event. The only difference is it missed ... If it had hit, we would still be picking up the pieces.'

But the truth is, Earth doesn't even need space to kill us. It's quite capable of doing that all on its own. Placed, as we are, in the middle of one big tectonic plate, and well away from all its tremoring edges, Australia doesn't really have any active volcanoes to speak of, and our earthquakes tend to be pretty mild. But it's worth our keeping an eye on Sumatra, the Indonesian island 2000 kilometres to our north-west. That's because it's home to a spot that's worth visiting one day, if you like your freshwater bodies to be nice and roomy. More than 100 kilometres long and 30 kilometres wide, Lake Toba is the largest lake in South-East Asia and one of the biggest in the whole world.

But here's the thing. Toba's not just a lake. That whole freaking thing is a freaking volcano. Essentially a crater so massive that it could not form a mountain, so instead made a hole in the ground, Lake Toba is the world's biggest supervolcano. It's generally thought to be in a stage of resurgence. 'We can see that this island is gradually increasing in height, indicating that the volcano is active and that magma is accumulating underneath,' says Ping-Ping Liu of Peking University.

Last time Toba erupted, 75,000 years ago, it produced enough ash to block out the sun. The result was a decades-long 'volcanic winter' that almost wiped out most life on Earth.

Point is: Toba won't just be bad news for Sumatrans if and when it decides to go off again. It will be bad news for us down here in Australia. It will be bad for everyone in the world. Vast quantities of sulphur dioxide will poison the atmosphere, along with blankets of soot, and hot rocks will rain down from the sky. Earthquakes will be triggered. Tsunamis will be caused. Temperatures will plummet and crops will be ruined. Only a few places on the planet will have clean drinking water. And they will each become settings for wars.

Any day that doesn't involve a natural disaster is a good and a lucky day. Even if you have to spend it in Moree.

Near Misses

Would-be assassins who didn't quite hit the mark

'Remember, democracy never lasts long. It soon wastes, exhausts, and murders itself. There never was a democracy yet that did not commit suicide.'

John Adams, US president and founding father

There comes a time in every person's life when, however young they may feel (deep down, on the inside), they start to sound kind of cranky and old. If the next two paragraphs provide any indication, my own time may well have come.

Back in the good old days, you see, keeping up with the news was quite different, insofar as there generally *was* some. Some actual developments that would affect how you lived, or reshape the world in some small way, shape or form. But nowadays most news outlets just churn out fatuous nonsense, in between clickbait and fluff. If you need to know what some WAG has been wearing, or the '10 reasons why you should (or should not) drink coffee', then most news websites will have what you're after, along with parenting tips, celebrity nip slips, amazing new diets and recent real estate trends.

All this 'dumbing down' is a bit of a drag, but it's worth keeping in mind that, on some level, it could also be seen as a bit of a privilege. Australia, all this banality rather suggests, is essentially a nation with not all that much to worry about. The simple fact of the matter is that, however gamely the Canberra press gallery tries to persuade us some story matters – however gamely they try to create conflict and drama and triumph and disaster out of a change in the polls or some minister's minor slip of the tongue – Australia's society is stable and Australia's economy is good. The whole political system hums along pretty smoothly. By and large, things are tickety-boo.

Now obviously none of this is to say that we don't have real problems and should not be hard at work trying to fix them. It's simply to say that we should have a sense of perspective. That by world standards, our issues are mild. Next time you're feeling strong, switch on the TV news. Right before the fifteen minutes of sport and weather, and some cute animal being born in a zoo, you'll see a one-minute montage of actual news, going on in a place far away. A montage featuring wars and assassinations and protests and violence. A cavalcade of coups and catastrophes.

Australia is a lucky country when it comes to this kind of stuff. But there have been times when we've come very to close it. Back in 1868, for example: a time when Britannia ruled the waves and the sun never set on her glorious empire. A time when the Australian colonies were under the thumb of Her Gracious Majesty, Queen Victoria, and keen to bend a knee when she sent us one of her sons.

On a royal tour of all the shitter colonies that his mum couldn't quite be arsed visiting, the twenty-three-year-old Prince Alfred Ernest Albert was not just the Duke of Edinburgh, the Earl of Ulster, the Earl of Kent, the future Duke of Saxe-Coburg and Gotha and second in line to the British throne. He was also, by all accounts, a bit of a party boy – a budding alcoholic who liked to get out and about, chat with his subjects and, with a bit of luck, go on to shag them.

While most Australians at the time were still loyal to the Crown and prepared to do their duty (in or out of the bedroom), we also had plenty of Ned Kelly types: Irish Catholics who actively hated the English and would much prefer us to be a republic. It was a real social divide but not such a deep one. Sectarian tensions were vivid and would remain for a century, but the occasional pub brawl, or rather brutal social snubbing, tended to be about as dramatic as the divide ever got. Politically speaking, things were quite stable. Our nascent democracy was in no way at threat.

But it very, very easily could have been if Henry O'Farrell had known how to handle a gun. A hard-drinking greengrocer from Ballarat who had spent some time in a mental asylum, O'Farrell was one of those Irish Catholic immigrants who firmly opposed British rule. So when the thirty-five-year-old discovered that Prince Alfred was soon due to appear at a charity picnic in Clontarf, he decided to buy a gun and join the 500-strong crowd in the hope that the famously gregarious prince would come up to shake a few hands.

Alfred did. So O'Farrell shot him. From just a few feet away.

The prince is dead, long live the prince? No. The prince did not die at all. O'Farrell's first shot went just to the right of the spine, and should by rights have ripped through a few organs. But more or less miraculously, the bullet glanced off a rib and only inflicted the most minor of wounds. O'Farrell's second shot, meanwhile, managed to miss altogether. It instead hit a bystander right in the foot, causing him to faint while the prince screamed in pain.

O'Farrell was getting ready to shoot a third time, but instead found himself being lynched by a mob. Stripped naked and 'battered to a pulp' by a crowd determined to 'string him up', the would-be assassin would have been assassinated himself had the police not managed drag him away. In any event, he was dead within weeks, after a judge saw no reason to not bring in the hangman.

But Australians can count themselves lucky that our democracy didn't die too, in the time it took for the prince to be released – clearly alive – from hospital. Just as 9/11 did Aussie Muslims no favours, Alfred's attempted assassination unleashed a tidal wave of social unrest, rampant racism and religious intolerance. Angry mobs attacked Irish-owned homes and businesses, while hundreds of angry meetings were held in town halls.

With so many voters denouncing 'Fenian terrorism', and politicians to 'defend British culture', leaders like NSW Colonial-Secretary Sir

Henry Parkes were more than happy to do the right thing. The right thing, of course, being pandering. Within just a week of the shooting, he rammed a *Treason Felony Act* through the NSW Parliament to ensure 'the better suppression and punishment of seditious practices and attempt'. So undemocratic as to be almost laughable, the bill didn't just seek to repress and punish people who used 'disrespectful' language about the Queen. It sought to repress and punish anyone who refused to drink a toast to her health or join in any 'loyal demonstration' organised in her honour.

In short, 'Australia descended into moral panic, shame, vengeance, bigotry and political division and opportunism,' to quote historian Steve Harris. Who knows what sorts of draconian lawmaking might have come next if the prince had not swiftly recovered and issued a call for calm. But because Australia's lucky, he did.

Or could it be that luck runs in the family? Because 102 years later, we had a similar stroke of luck with Prince Alfred's great-great-grand-niece – a lady better known as Queen Elizabeth II. By 1970, the British Empire was not quite what it had been (much like Russel Brand's career now). This meant that the monarch was no longer in a position to fob us off with junior royals in search of a shag. This meant that this time, she had to come here herself. She had to press lots of flesh, wave at some crowds and feign interest in whatever crap we could show her.

On 30 April the Queen was in a whitegoods factory in Orange, smiling and nodding while someone showed her some fridges and doing her best to try to think of a question.

But as bad as this sounds, this wasn't the worst part of her day. Because only that morning, she had come close to death. According to local police, the royal train that Her Majesty was travelling to Orange in could and should have come loose as it hurtled at speed through the nearby Blue Mountains. Not because the engine was faulty, or the driver was bad. But because someone had placed a log on the tracks.

'You can't say outright that it was an attempt to kill the Queen but it could well have been,' said Superintendent Cliff McHardy, who kept the story secret for more than forty years. 'It [the log] was about six foot to seven foot, about eight inches to nine inches diameter; enough to put a train off rails. We were told that if [the train] was going at full speed it would have derailed it.'

Unfortunately for what was either a half-arsed assassin or a very whole-hearted prankster, the royal train never hit the log at high speed. In fact, it never hit it at all. It turns out that the federal police were also the fun police and had sent out an advance train to scout out any threat. They even got it to move super slowly so as to be able to spot danger, which meant that it wasn't even really damaged when it hit the log.

At least you couldn't have accused them of being overly solicitous about Arthur Calwell when he was attacked just a few years before. The leader of the federal Labor party during the 1960s – a thankless period that saw them remain stuck in opposition, just as they had been throughout the whole 1950s – Calwell was an old-timer socialist, a staunch Irish Catholic and an ardent opponent of conscription and war. Somewhat less attractively, he was also less than keen on multiculturalism. He's mostly remembered today (if he's ever remembered at all) for insisting that 'two Wongs do not make a white'.

But back on 21 June 1966, he was very much a national celebrity. And with a federal election scheduled for later that year, there was every reason to believe that he would soon be PM. When the then 69-year-old went to a rally at the Mosman Town Hall to rail against the war in Vietnam he drew quite a big crowd. More than 800 people came along to cheer, clap and generally voice their support – though it turned out this support was not entirely unanimous.

Close observers started to sense this at about 10.45pm, when the rally had largely wound up. After shaking hands with a few dozen well-wishers and exchanging waves with a few dozen more, Calwell finally managed to make his way through the crowd and get into his Commonwealth car. But there are always more voters to meet, greet and woo when an election is just a few months away. So the Labor leader dutifully began to wind down his window to unleash some more charm when he saw a young man approach.

But it turned out that this man was not a well-wisher. He was a would-be assassin. Undoing his overcoat, he produced a sawn-off shotgun and fired at Calwell from less than three feet away. The Labor leader should have died then and there. His face should have exploded in a burst of red mist. His headless body should have slumped to the floor.

But, by a stroke of good luck, Calwell hadn't finished winding down the extra-strong window of his Commonwealth car. Which meant that the bullet clipped the top and was diverted off course, instead of making a hole through his chin.

'There was an exploding sound [and] I felt a stinging sensation to the front of my face,' said the matter-of-fact socialist, after spending just one night in hospital to remove a few small shards of glass. He was back up and campaigning within the week – a period that gave him just enough time to lead Labor to yet another horrible loss, and be replaced by Gough Whitlam.

His attacker was equally fortunate. A nineteen-year-old factory worker and 'borderline schizophrenic', Peter Kocan didn't particularly care about politics. He just wanted to kill a public figure, like the late Lee Harvey Oswald, who'd become a household name after he shot JFK.

> Unless I did something out of the ordinary I realized I would remain a nobody all my life. I came to the conclusion that however hard it was I would have to do something that would set me apart from other nobodies. I would not have done anything so cruel as shoot someone if I had any alternative.

As logic goes, this seems less than watertight, but it was apparently good enough for the authorities. Sentenced to just ten years in jail, Kocan spent his time studying history, philosophy and literature, and publishing a small volume of poems. After his release, he went on to enjoy a distinguished career in the arts, writing award-winning novels and earning some weighty degrees.

All in all, quite a nice story, I'd say. I wonder whether it ever made the news.

Flying High

Aussies who fell from the sky and survived

'If God had really intended men to fly, he'd have made it easier to get to the airport.'

George Winters, US actor

I'm not a person to needlessly nitpick or point out minor flaws in a song, but in the interests of public health and safety, I think it needs to be pointed out that R Kelly was wrong in 'I Believe I Can Fly'. Whatever he may 'believe' to the contrary, that R&B superstar cannot in fact 'fly'. Let alone 'touch the sky'. And nor can I, you or anyone else. That whole 'spread my wings' line is a metaphor, at best. Or maybe some kind of simile.

Bottom line: human beings were designed to stay on the ground, which makes our attempts to fly somewhat problematic. Henri L'Estrange, however, had no reservations. Born in Melbourne back in 1842, and seemingly keen to get this whole 'being alive' thing over and done with, he became a tightrope walker at the age of thirty-six, after some unsuccessful stints as a gymnast and dancer.

'With his rope suspended 40 feet above the ground,' wrote one spectator, 'L'Estrange walked backwards and forwards, walked in armour, walked covered in a sack, used and sat on a chair, cooked and rode a bicycle, all on the rope. His show then finished with a fireworks display for the public's entertainment.'

What could possibly go wrong? The answer was clearly 'a lot'. L'Estrange was eventually forced into yet another career change when some sparks from a firework hit an open crate full of gunpowder and caused a gigantic explosion that burnt down his tent. Several spectators were injured in the stampede to escape, partly because they had to break down a fence.

Clearly, the showman needed to start taking safety more seriously. So he decided to start flying hot air balloons. At that time, a very new form of transport. And very, very far from a safe one.

Equipped with equally novel technology, like sandbags and a parachute, L'Estrange's first attempt did not go especially well, insofar as he crashed into a train. But that wasn't such a problem, as the train wasn't moving at the time, and his balloon had barely managed to get 20 feet from the ground.

Attempt number two was more successful, insofar as this time he managed to get 50 feet into the air. But it was also less successful, insofar as he could not come down. A tricky problem that he eventually solved by crashing into a homeless shelter.

Having somehow managed to survive that crash, too, L'Estrange started to rethink his life choices ... and decided that his next crash ought to take place in Melbourne. After soaring hundreds of feet above the Flemington Showgrounds, he became the first Australian to use an emergency parachute when his balloon burst into flames. And he really should have become the first Australian to *die* using a parachute except for a stroke of luck that saw a tree break his fall.

Clearly, this whole ballooning thing was completely insane. So L'Estrange decided to do it again. March 1881 therefore saw him soar hundreds and hundreds of feet above Sydney ... take in the views ... revel in the moment ... and discover a mechanical problem that meant he couldn't steer.

> Picture to yourself my horror when I found the escape valve would not act. I tried with all the strength of the one hand I had to spare to move it, for with the other I had to hold myself in the loop of rope, but all to no purpose, it would not budge an inch. In sheer desperation I took the valve rope in both hands, and it opened with a bang; but in the effort I had lost my seat in the loop, falling about six feet, and there I was dangling in mid-air, clutching the valve rope, the gas rushing out of the balloon as though she had burst.

And burst the balloon eventually did, just 50 feet above Woolloomooloo. Bright enough to 'cast a brief but vivid illumination over the entire suburb', the explosion permanently blinded one resident, burnt a few more, and caused many to be injured in a panicked stampede.

But don't you worry, reader: Henri L'Estrange was just fine. Right as rain, if not even righter. After managing to disentangle himself from the valve rope, the showman was able to drop just 25 feet down onto a conveniently placed chimney seconds before his balloon crashed into the house right next door and burnt it down to the ground.

His ballooning career, though, took a bit of a hit. 'Reputation in tatters', the performer was finally forced to give flying away and make his long-dreaded return to the stage. A little annoyingly, he went on to live to a ripe old age ... fortunately dying just a few years before 1903, when Orville Wright became the first person to ever fly a plane.

Naturally enough, Orville also went on to become the first person to ever crash a plane – and the fatal collisions certainly haven't stopped there. Famous people to lose their life flying include Buddy Holly, Ritchie Valens and the Big Bopper (the 50s rockers immortalised in the song 'American Pie'); the musicians Patsy Cline, John Denver and Otis Redding; the basketballer Kobe Bryant; the boxer Rocky Marciano; and the Soviet cosmonaut Yuri Gagarin. Plus of course Australia's own 'Shirley' Strachan, the much-loved frontman for Skyhooks.

But with a pinch of good luck and a hint of sheer arse, not every plane crash actually has to be deadly. A few ordinary Australians have become famous themselves for somehow finding a way to emerge from one fully intact. Take Joseph Binstead, for example: a Manly man and a manly man who became a household name for doing just that, along with a Mr John Proud.

Binstead, Proud and a Mr Jim Westray were among the seven passengers aboard a small Stinson aeroplane on a 1937 flight from Brisbane to Sydney. Forced to make a dramatic detour inland when a storm hit the east coast, the plane flew several hundred kilometres west of its prearranged route – and then headed due south. By which I mean that it crashed to the ground, immediately killing four souls onboard.

Miraculously, Binstead, Westray and Proud survived the crash with only a few burns, bruises and one broken leg. But as day turned into night, and then into day, they began to realise that the dead passengers may have in fact been the lucky ones. Because not only did they not know where they were; the rest of the world had no idea, either.

Where they were was, in essence, the middle of nowhere: a vast and dense stretch of rainforest 800 kilometres from Sydney. A rainforest so free of people – so pristine, so remote – that it had become one of Australia's first national parks a few decades before.

This was a problem because, while the plane's disappearance led to nationwide headlines and one of the biggest land, sea and air searches in Australian history, said searches were mostly focused just north of Sydney, thanks to several (completely incorrect) 'sightings'. After seven long days of following false leads, the authorities finally called off the search, convinced that the plane must have been lost at sea.

By this time, a severely burnt Westray had already limped off from the wreckage to try to find help – and, in the process, fallen to his death off a cliff. Proud's broken leg had left him unable to move (though you'll be glad to know that 'a growing colony of maggots ... ultimately saved the limb'), so Binstead elected to stay by the twisted, black wreck of the plane and fetch him water from a nearby creek. Food, however, was nowhere to be found, and by the time that a full ten days had gone by, the two were both just about ready for a cliff jump themselves.

But cometh the moment cometh the man – the man in this case being Bernard O'Reilly. His family had built a house in the rainforest just before it became a park and spent the next thirty years refusing to leave it. But he was not just one of those men who don't bow to peer pressure. He was also one of those men who don't believe what they read.

He did, however, occasionally believe what he heard. The day after authorities declared the plane lost, O'Reilly's brother told him that he wasn't surprised that the plane hadn't been found down near Sydney. Reason being, he was pretty sure that he'd seen it himself, flying by on the day of the storm. And he was pretty sure it had been heading west.

Now it's worth noting that 'eyewitness sightings' were hardly rare at the time. Pretty much every second person between Brisbane and Sydney was pretty sure that they'd seen the plane that day too. The only rational response was to change the subject, avoid eye contact and back away, nice and slow.

Bernard O'Reilly, however, was a bit of an idiot. Taking his brother at his word, he set off on foot the following day through the endless expanse of thick, green, dense forest. Two days and about 40 kilometres later, he reached the top of a high mountain – and proved that he was, in fact, smart.

> For 15 minutes, I stood in cool moist wind, looking into a grey blank, and then suddenly the racing clouds split, and a vast green sea of ranges and gorges came into view to the west. Here and there were creamy white splashes which I knew to be trees in bloom, and then I saw something which made me jump.
>
> Eight miles away by the map, on the third range, Lamington Plateau, just where it swelled up to join the border range, was a treetop which was light brown. The tree must have been dying; what had caused that? Natural causes? No; trees dying that way die a branch at a time. Fire? No natural fire had occurred in that dripping rainforest since the world began. But a hundred gallons of petrol [might do the trick].

Setting out on an eight-hour hike to investigate further, he finally came upon 'a horrible, unclean thing, which held the remains of what once were men'. And two very much alive men weakly slumped alongside it.

How lucky were they?

Obviously, pretty lucky. But let's face it, they'd still had a bad week. A much better way to survive a plane crash, in my humble opinion, is to not actually be in the plane. And if you don't believe me, just ask the much-travelled Ted Woodbry. A jetsetting businessman who lived and worked on the Gold Coast, he was all set to jet from Vermont to Boston in July 1973 when a thick fog led to a hold-up in traffic, causing him to just miss his plane. Which was infuriating, of course, but also allowed him to miss one of the worst airline disasters in all human history. Delta Air Lines flight 723 famously crashed on landing, killing all eighty-nine folks on board.

And that wasn't the only flight that Woodbry missed, as the then ninety-year-old told the *Gold Coast Bulletin* in 2019. In the early 80s, he was in Florida, patiently waiting for a helicopter but becoming ever less patient as it failed to arrive. It turned out that it had an underlying mechanical problem that had caused it to crash en route. 'The helicopter hit [an] apartment block and [was] wrecked,' he recalled. 'Luckily no one was injured, but I caught the taxi.'

Woodbry's luck turned in 1985, a year that finally saw him get to the airport and board a flight without incident. Getting off the flight was a little more problematic, however, given that it had crashed into Port Macquarie. 'We'd taken off and reached a height of about 10 storeys and the alarm went off,' he recalls of the accident, which left him with bad spinal injuries. 'The pilot lowered wing flaps, we crashed into a paddock and the impact point was on my actual seat. A passenger kicked the rear door out, fuel was leaking, most passengers travelled about 15 metres from the wreck and were on the ground.'

'The gentleman beside me was bleeding badly from the neck, so I covered the neck area for over 40 minutes while on my knees.

Passengers were placed in an ambulance, there was no room for me, so I travelled in the front seat with the driver.'

There was also not all that much room at the local hospital, where Woodbry was forced to stay for the next several weeks. A few days in, he recalls, 'The top specialist told me I had to be out by 9.30am, they need the bed [but] the nurse said I wasn't going anywhere, so she went and got the matron, who arranged for a special test.'

Said medical test found that he had five blood clots in his lungs – blood clots that could well have preceded the crash. Blood clots that would not have been discovered without it.

'They told me I would have been dead within 24 hours,' he said.

Maybe flying *is* actually a good idea after all.

PART THREE

THE WHEEL OF FORTUNE

Some people tell their children not to talk to strangers, but for mine that is only the start.

I also advise them not to talk to rugby players. Or fashion designers. Or meditators. Or DJs. Or anyone who doesn't know the difference between 'there', 'their' and 'they're'. People who brew their own beer are clearly a no-no, and the same goes for anyone who quotes lines from the Simpsons or likes to post things on LinkedIn. And don't even get me started on people who talk about their 'stars' (or, even worse, their cars). Or who have ever once used the phrase 'OMG'.

Now it may be that judgemental people are also worth shunning. But in my judgement, 'self-made' ones are worse. I am of course talking about the Gina Rineharts of this world – the dynamic go-getters who were able to become billionaires after their parents left them barely $100 mill. The wealthy types who owe the world nothing (least of all tax) because they got where they were through hard work.

'I make my own luck' is the sort of thing that they might say if they weren't so busy firing some minion. Capitalism is a game that rewards skill and hard work – and it's very clearly a game that they're great at.

Well ... maybe. In some ways. Just a bit. Now and then.

But like all games, capitalism tends to be unfair. Some players strike out through no fault of their own, while others are essentially born on third base. Some people get injured, or don't know the rules. And some people ignore the rules altogether.

And I don't need to add that some people get lucky. Because you'll see this yourself, if you just turn the page.

The Luck of the Draw

Aussies who hit the jackpot

'I've done the calculation and your chances of winning the lottery are identical whether you play or not.'

Fran Lebowitz, New York author

Have you ever 'done a ginger' or been 'as crook as Rookwood'? 'Humped the swag' or 'gone off your kadoova'?

Sorry, no, I don't know what I'm talking about either. Back in the day, Australia was full of quaint little phrases that have all since gone to buggery. They're clanked out; cactus; as dead as a dingo. Try using them today and you'll find that they're not worth a cracker. People will think that you're a penny short of the pound, and you'll be about as popular as a Polly Waffle in a public pool. True blue. I would not tell a furphy.

Anyway, enough of all that. Where were we? Oh yes: another useful phrase to hit the frog and toad was 'the luck of Eric Connolly'. A famous name in the racing community, which a hundred years ago basically meant all of Australia, Connolly was a horse owner, trainer and punter from country Victoria whose whole career seemed to be one big, long winning streak. Said streak began at age twenty-three, when he bought an 'undistinguished' sprinter for practically nothing, only for it to immediately win the Grand National. His ostensible 'long-shots' also won at Oakleigh, Williamstown, Newmarket and the Metropolitan – and even took down Phar Lap to win the 1929 Melbourne Cup. Regarded as 'Australia's outstanding better' according to journalist John Debiase, 'punters eagerly awaited his presence, always looking for clues on what Connolly found good to bet on the day'.

Perhaps a better phrase, however, would be 'the luck of Robert Packer'. The founder of a billion-dollar media dynasty, this small-time Tassie journalist would have remained a small-time Tassie journalist were it not for a huge stroke of luck. According to his grandson Kerry, the Packer dynasty kicked off during a day at the Hobart Races back in 1902, when Robert happened to find a ten-shilling note lying right on the ground. Not one to look a gift horse in the mouth, the twenty-three-year-old bet it all on a twelve-to-one long shot – a twelve-to-one long shot that of course cantered home.

'He bought a ticket to Sydney and went into the newspaper industry and did quite well,' Kerry would say. 'That's where my family started from: 10-bob on a racecourse.'

Or maybe we should be saying 'the luck of Kev Cain'? That unemployed Melbourne punter had only $10 to his name when he woke on Show Day back in 1978. It probably hadn't been such a great sleep, because he couldn't afford to buy a bed – or indeed any other furniture to fill the flat that he could not afford and from which he was about to be evicted.

But with that $10, Kev could at least afford a couple of beers, so he brushed his teeth and headed down to the pub. The plan was to meet a friend and get a lift to Caulfield Racecourse, where he would try to borrow a little money and maybe place a few bets. But the friend was running late, so a couple of $2 beers in, Cain turned his attention to the races on the telly. And decided to place his final $6 on a thirty-three-to-one shot.

As chance would have it, it cantered home, as Andrew Rule writes in a book called, um, *Chance*:

> So away he goes. Then he sees an 11–2 shot ... about a $5 bet. He's watching it on the board, and it gets pushed into 5–1 and then into 9–2, so obviously there's money for it. So he jumps on and puts his 200 bucks on it, and it wins. You don't have to be told he goes from horse to horse to horse and keeps winning.

By the final race, Cain had won no less than $86,000. Enough, way back then, to buy a nice house and even fill it with plenty of furniture. But he instead 'spent the money on wine, women and song'.

Sadly, such behaviour has always been thus – Australians have been ardent gamblers ever since the First Fleet. In fact, as one visitor to the colony observed, 'to such excesses was the pursuit of gambling carried [out] among the convicts that some have been known, after losing money, provisions, and all their clothing, to have staked their clothes upon their wretched backs, standing in the midst of their associates naked ...' Gambling-related nudity may not be super common today, but the average Australian is still said to lose more than $1200 from betting every single year – a stat that makes us the world's biggest gamblers by a considerable margin. Or, if you prefer, the world's worst.

Perhaps the smart money is actually in *buying* a horse, rather than placing a bet? That would certainly be the view of Michael Achurch. A tattoo-strewn gardener from a less-than-affluent Sydney suburb, Achurch had a big day at the track back in 2002, scooping up around $7000. Later that afternoon, however, he saw an ad for an unraced two-year-old filly, which was selling for $6950 a share. 'I didn't know anything about horses, their breeding, nothing,' the twenty-two-year-old father later recalled. 'I just thought it would be a bit of fun to own a racehorse.'

This hunch turned out to be quite correct. Achurch's cheapo horse promptly won the 2003 Golden Slipper, the world's richest race for two-year olds, and went to be sold on for more than $2 million. What do you do with money like that? Why not just go out and buy another horse? So, Achurch did. And watched it win the Cox Plate.

'Some people are born under a lucky star,' says racehorse guru Dean Watt. 'Everything Michael Achurch touches turns to gold. Some people have pig's feet for luck, we've got "group 1 Mick". He's a lucky charm.'

Mick happily agrees.

> I've just been lucky. Both horses have been big odds when they have won and the family has had some good wins. Some people can whack away for years, sometimes spending millions, and get nothing more than a winner of a country maiden. Getting a good horse is like winning the lottery.

Want to know what else is like winning the lottery? Winning the lottery. And if you don't believe me, just ask the unemployed cleaner who took home $80 million in 2021, after winning the Division One Powerball. A household name that no one can name, because he chose to remain anonymous, the middle-aged North Melbourne dad had a one-in-134,000 chance of picking the right combination of numbers, but that was all he required.

'I am so excited. I checked my ticket late last night. I couldn't sleep after that!' the family man told Channel 7 News.

> I lost my job during one of the many lockdowns here in Melbourne. We had only just bought a home and didn't see it coming. I've been working as a cleaner ever since to make ends meet. Like for so many people, these lockdowns have been really tough for our family. But I've always said, you've just gotta keep trying.

Or alternatively, you can just make a mistake. In 2017, another anonymous Victorian – this time from Point Cook – accidentally managed to win TattsLotto twice. 'At first, I thought "wow I've won $1.3 million" so at first, I was lying in bed shaking,' he told journalists after the win. 'But then after an hour or so I realised I hadn't checked the rest of my tickets so I looked at the next one and to my surprise I found that I'd played the same game twice [online]. I wasn't expecting to win once, let alone twice.'

But the luckiest two-time winner is clearly Bill Morgan – because he also won a new lease of life. A truck driver who lived in a caravan park somewhere on the outskirts of Melbourne, Morgan may not have had wealth but he at least had his health. Until he was involved in a massive car crash at age thirty-seven.

Rushed to hospital in a critical condition, after being dragged unconscious from the crumpled wreck of his truck, Morgan's condition was so urgent that the doctors used all they could to revive him, despite not having a medical history on hand. A decision that, in retrospect, may have been a mistake, as the one of drugs that they used caused an allergic reaction.

And by an allergic reaction, I don't mean a nasty red rash or some itchy red eyes or a sneeze that stuck around for three days. I mean that his heart just stopped pumping.

Generally speaking, the term 'clinically dead' is replaced by 'officially dead' after about seven minutes. That's about how long it takes for your brain to shut down once your heart has stopped sending it oxygen. So it's unclear why the doctors persisted with their resuscitation attempts for fourteen long minutes – why they frantically continued to pump away at a patient who was, officially speaking, a corpse.

Whatever the answer might have been, it's clear that their persistence paid off. Morgan's heartbeat returned at the fifteenth minute and, now officially alive, he lapsed into a coma.

Eleven days later, he was still in a coma and still showing no signs of improvement. Was his brain working or was it now complete mush? Was he still Bill or some kind of crazed anti-vaxxer? Concerned that he would either die very soon, or essentially spend his life as a vegetable, Morgan's doctors again and again advised his family members to switch off life support. And every single time, his family members refused.

All of which, one imagines, would have made for a slightly awkward scene, when the 'one-in-a-million' patient miraculously woke up on day twelve with a brain in perfectly good working order. It was, as one of his sheepish doctors declared, nothing less than 'a medical miracle'.

But even medical miracles still have bills to pay, and Bill wasn't quite well enough to go back to work. So, once he was out of hospital, a month or so later, one of his first moves was to invest in a $5 scratchie. And wouldn't you know it, it won him a car. A brand-new Toyota Corolla.

You can say all sorts of things about commercial news outlets, but you can't ever accuse them of not being cheesy. Bill's heart-warming story was fluff sent by God to fill in the two minutes before sport and weather. 'Back from the dead' plus 'Rags to riches' clearly equalled a perfect way to fill time during the next slow news day, so when word of Bill's recovery and car win leaked out, a Channel 9 news crew was quick to get in touch.

Needing some good footage now that Bill was awake and bruise-free, they sent him to his local newsagent with TV cameras in tow, so he could re-enact the moment that he bought the scratchie.

While he was there, they thought he may as well get a shot of him scratching it too, in case they needed some more stuff for a voiceover. It was a good plan, I think, but a plan that was ruined when Bill suddenly gave a start and spoke up.

'I just won $250,000.'

Lucky Finds

Aussies who found hidden treasure

'We must believe in luck. For how else can we explain the success of those we don't like?'

Jean Cocteau, French poet

True wealth, said the Buddha, lies in contentment – in a life filled with peace, health and love.

There may or may not be some truth in this theory but it's clearly in need of some work. True wealth, you see, can also lie on the beach. Just ask Leon and Loralee Wright.

Back in 2006, you see, these middle-aged South Australians were walking along a remote beach not far from Streaky Bay when they came across a grey and slightly odd-looking tree stump. On closer inspection, however, it proved to be something else. Something waxy and misshapen and weirdly light for its size. Something that was strange, gross and stinky.

Thinking that it might well be some kind of whale cyst, Leon suggested that they take it home. Agreeing that it might well be some kind of whale cyst, Loralee very naturally refused. Being the wife, Loralee won the argument, and the couple continued on their walk without it.

They remained curious, however, after getting home from their holiday, and eventually emailed a marine ecologist to find out what it was. He told them that they may well have found a big chunk of ambergris and suggested that they hightail it back to the beach. A kind of hard, smelly mucous that sperm whales spew up, ambergris may not look or sound all that great, but in the right hands it can apparently produce a great smell. Pretty much *the* key ingredient in pricey perfumes, just a tiny little slice of what's essentially whale vomit can bring in about $300,000.

'Lucky for us, the high tide didn't pick it up and the wind carry it back to sea,' said Leon of the 14 kilogram grey lump that was still sitting right where they'd seen it. 'And, like, when we saw it – because you could see [it] very way off – yeah, we even got more excited. We were sort of dancing and clapping and cheering on the beach like we were very excited.'

But that's enough talk about vomit and mucous. Let's talk about toilets instead. Or more specifically, let's talk about a toilet at Channel 9 studios in Melbourne; a toilet that may or may not be familiar to people who like to buy or sell coke. I cast no aspersions, of course. I merely note that it was also a toilet that happened to have $100,000 worth of banknotes hidden in a sanitary bin and down the pipes. A small fortune that precisely nobody laid claim to on 9 May 2014, the day it was discovered by a cleaner.

'There was too much to count, I thought someone was playing a prank on me,' said Chamindu Amarsinghe. 'But when I touched the notes – all yellow and green – I realised it was real money.' It was also *his* money, the Melbourne Magistrates' Court later decided, on the grounds that the cleaner and part-time IT student had immediately reported the find to police. 'There's no reason why such honesty should go unrewarded.'

A more traditional way to strike gold is to, well, strike gold: to poke about for a nugget with a spade, pick or pan. According to writer Christina Sexton, worldwide, it's said that 'more gold was discovered between 1848 and the end of the 19th century than in the previous 3000 years' – and it goes without saying that a lot of it came from down under. A remarkable stroke of good luck for a sparsely populated little colony that was still not too much more than a prison, the 1850s gold rush did not just put Australians on a path to prosperity, it dragged us all the way down the road. With 2500 tonnes flowing from Victoria alone, Australia's rivers of gold led to new roads and railways, new shops and factories, new telegraph lines and industrialised farms. Minor ports became major cities. Random fields became quaint little towns. Migrants came here from all over the world, quadrupling the population in less than two decades.

But the rivers of gold did not always run very evenly. For every miner who managed to 'strike it lucky', there were many more who toiled away in the sun with no result whatsoever – unless you count back pain and skin cancer and crippling debt, a touch of scurvy and a case of black lung. As an Italian migrant of the time observed, 'Ballarat was a Nugety [sic] Eldorado for the few [and] a ruinous field of hard labour for many.'

John Deason and Richard Oates are two good examples. By 1869, they had dug for eight years in the dirt and the rocks without finding anything except rocks and dirt. 'Disheartened and disillusioned' but determined to continue, the two Cornishmen decided to head further south. After a few days on a wagon, they decided to try their luck in Moliagul, a former boom town that had been 'energetically and profitably worked' for some years. Most miners had thought it 'played out' and moved on. Today, it's just a handful of farms.

But, wouldn't you know it, they found a nugget in no time at all. A nugget lying underneath just three centimetres of soil in a 'well-established (digging) area' just 2 kilometres out of town. And when I say a nugget, I of course mean *the* nugget. The 'Welcome Stranger', AKA the biggest one ever found. A 97 kilogram chunk of gold that actually had to be broken up before being valued, because it was far too big to ever fit on the scales.

How did Deason and Oates instantly find what so many had missed? Well, in truth, it is hard to be sure. But the story goes that the Stranger was buried just on the edge of a busy wagon trail, tucked away amid the roots of a tree. A public place, of sort, that no one would ever choose to dig, unless they wanted to get into an argument with wagoners about twelve times a day. Legend has it that Deason only decided to dig there because of a lucky accident: his wagon wheels had slightly slipped off the track and in the process exposed a slight gleam.

Goldmining today does not give us stories like this. Dame Fortune barely seems to feature at all. It's a much more specialised and scientific enterprise involving soulless corporations and more soulless people – plus cranes and scoops and trucks and haulers, and armies of geologists who actually know what they're doing. William Howitt may have been right 150 years ago when he said mining was 'a lottery, with far more blanks than prizes', but in this day and age you're more or less guaranteed to strike it rich ... so long as you are already so rich you don't actually need to.

The Hilliers, however, were quite far from rich. In fact, they were really quite poor. Travelling around Australia in a battered old van, this family of six relied on the father, Kevin, to find the occasional odd job as a handyman. But after sustaining a nasty back injury in 1980, Kevin was no longer able to do manual labour, or even sit for long in a car. The deeply religious family was forced to set up base in Bridgewater, an old Victorian gold town, and pray that their luck would soon change.

'We had no worker's compensation at that time, no money and no income,' Kevin's wife Bep recalls. 'I was cleaning toilets in the caravan park so that we could stay there for free. People who were leaving the next day would come to me with food, potatoes, tomatoes, meat, and say can you use this? They could not know how welcome that was!'

Rather less welcome was a local doctor's advice that the still-recovering Kev take a walk every day. But he dutifully obeyed because nothing is more important than health. And took a metal detector along because wealth is good too. Armed with this equipment, the invalid dared to dream, and I really do mean that, quite literally. On 9 September 1980, Hillier had a dream that he would soon find a nugget. A long, thin nugget that pointed up at the sky, then thickened out, not unlike a palm with the index finger raised.

Ten days later, he found it.

'I had my headphones on, but I heard something, and it took me a while before I realised it was Kevin screaming for me: "Darling! Darling!"' said Bep.

> I thought 'Oh no, something's happened,' and I went to look for him. He was on the ground, crying. I've never seen him like that before. He had a big hole in front of him, about 14 inches wide, and you could just see a bit of gold. And he said 'Darling, we're filthy rich,' and I'm praying, I'm praying to God!

Valued at roughly $5 million, and now on display in a Las Vegas casino, that 27 kilogram lump is one of the world's largest nuggets. The Hilliers called it 'The Hand of Faith'.

Another good name for buried treasure is the 'Black Star of Queensland'. It certainly beats 'crappy doorstop'. But when twelve-year-old Roy Spencer went for a walk in the remote, dusty hills around

Anakie back in 1938 and came home with what looked like 'a great lump of coal,' his gem-mining father, Harry, saw nothing more valuable than a largish black crystal. A geological oddity that was not valuable enough to be worth cutting down. But a geological oddity that, on balance, was probably worth keeping, because the family needed a doorstop.

It remained a doorstop for the next nine long years. Nine hot, punishing and not remotely prosperous years, in which Harry Spencer tried to find gems in this remote stretch of Queensland – but apparently didn't try too hard to find out more about them. In 1947, however, the cavalry arrived in the form of an unusually enterprising jewellery merchant from Los Angeles. Having taken it upon himself to cross the Pacific on the off-chance he could find stuff to sell, Harry Kazanjian alerted the Spencer family to an important fact: sapphires can actually come in all sorts of colours. They aren't just red (i.e. rubies) or clear. Hearing this, Spencer asked his wife to fetch the family doorstop. And discovered that the family had struck it rich.

Currently valued at around $100 million, the 733-carat Black Star of Queensland is the largest black sapphire that has ever been found. Famously worn by the singer, Cher, during a (not great) skit on her (even worse) TV show, it can now be seen at the Smithsonian Institution in Washington DC, in a star-shaped pendant encrusted with diamonds.

Good things, it seems, can sometimes happen to good people.

Though for bad people, the same rule applies. For a slightly less heartwarming tale of gemstone discovery, you need look no further than Kerry Packer. 'Extraordinarily evil' and 'morally corrupt', according to one former colleague and fan, this brothel-owning, big-game-hunting media mogul inherited a $100 million media empire from his just-as-vile dad in 1974. That empire would probably have been worth $10 billion by the time he died, if he'd just sold up straight away, bought an S&P share portfolio and spent the next thirty years on the beach. But he decided to work hard, day and night, at being a tycoon instead, and ended up with a little over $6 billion.

Even that figure owed a bit to good luck. The first came in the form of the Hawke government's decision to deregulate the television industry: a decision that financial analysts described as 'a one-billion-dollar gift entirely free of tax'.

The second came in the form of Alan Bond: a ludicrously overconfident businessman who bought Packer's Channel 9 at a 'crazy boom prize'. 'You only get one Alan Bond in your lifetime and I've had mine,' Packer said, after receiving more than $1 billion in exchange for his network ... and buying it back for a quarter of that price after Bond promptly went bankrupt.

With windfalls like this, Packer wasn't just able to buy more yachts and jets and a penthouse for his mistress. He was also able to buy a place to breed horses for polo. Featuring a sprawling mansion, several pools, a go-cart track, a cinema and a golf course, Packer's 30,000-hectare stud farm was already quite a nice place back in 1998. But it became even nicer the following year, when sapphires were found buried beneath it.

Ranging in colour from red to pink, and still being dug up to this day, the total find was valued at tens of millions.

Breathe in. Breathe out. Take a moment to sigh. Then sigh again, because things are about to get worse.

For all Kerry Packer's many faults – which include trying to break the worldwide sports boycott on Apartheid South Africa and threatening employees with a gun – he never actually called for Australia's Indigenous peoples to be sterilised, so they could 'breed themselves out'. *That*, of course, was Australian iron ore magnate Lang Hancock. Staunchly opposed to taxes and social welfare, since 'the best way to help the poor is not to become one of them', that crazy right-winger was also in favour of using nuclear weapons to make mining easier – though he didn't mind using people when it came to mining asbestos. As Larry Graham, MP for Pilbara, pointed out in 2002, 'Half a century after it was widely known that working with blue asbestos caused serious, life-threatening and terminal diseases, the Hancock family still had employees working in the mine. It took a specific Act of this Parliament to cease those operations.'

But it was iron ore, of course, that made this crazy man crazy-rich – and continues to enrich his equally likeable daughter. He famously found the world's largest deposit of the stuff in a remote, barren stretch of the remote, barren Pilbara. A lonely, desolate patch of desert about 1200 kilometres north of Perth, about 1400 kilometres south-west of Darwin and far, far away from anything resembling a town or a road.

How did he find it? The answer is luck. Or luck plus a pinch of bad weather.

In November 1952, Hancock was piloting a small plane from his asbestos mines in the north all the way down to Perth, when a storm forced him to detour through a gorge. 'Flying low, I followed the gorge,' he remembered. 'I noticed the walls. They were made of iron ore, but I figured it had to be poor grade. At the time, they said Australia didn't have any grade iron ore ... (but) I followed the iron ore in the walls for 70 miles.'

What a wonderful story for people named Lang. Let's hope that hell has iron ore.

A Sporting Chance

Aussie athletes who got a bit lucky

'Luck means a lot in football. Not having a good quarterback is bad luck.'

Don Shula, American football player

'I've never met a world champion that's a normal person,' says the world champion yachtsman, John Bertrand. 'You gotta be screwed up in some manner to get out of bed to do extraordinary things ... And I'm screwed up. Underneath this veneer of being a normal, nice guy, I have a huge ego. And the ego is part of my drive.'

As theories go, this one seems pretty sound – though it's worth remembering that if a huge ego was all it took to be great at sport, Bernard Tomić would have about twenty-seven Wimbledons by now, not just a crap haircut and all the charm of a haemorrhoid. Winning also requires work and a whole heap of talent.

And a bit of luck can be helpful as well.

John Bertrand, for example, might not have won the America's Cup back in 1983 were it not for a late lucky breeze. The first non-American boat to take the trophy in 132 years, his *Australia II* famously came from behind to beat Dennis Conner's *Liberty* in the seventh and final race of the tournament. Eighteen miles into the 24-mile course, on an unusually placid and still stretch of ocean, *Australia II* was almost a full minute behind its highly fancied US rival. That's an eternity, in yacht racing. It's like being down 6-0, 6-0, 5-0 in tennis, to put it in terms that Tomić would understand.

Bertrand's sailors had done their best, but – just like an Australian-made film – the result wasn't quite up to scratch. And that, my friend, really should have been that, in any just, sane and reasonable world.

In *this* world, however, *Liberty* suddenly chose to veer left, in search of something resembling a breeze. Our boys, for some reason, chose to stay right – and were immediately rewarded with a huge gust of wind. An almighty breeze that basically came out of nowhere and sped them straight to the finish line. 'In many ways Dennis Conner should have won but lady luck smiled on us,' said *Australia II*'s owner, Alan Bond. 'It is still hard to imagine where that breeze came from that got us over the line.'

Still an iconic moment in sports-mad Australia, the 'race of the century' was somewhat less well-received by the Americans, who questioned the legality of Bertrand's winged keel. 'Handsome heartthrob' John Devitt had similar troubles at the 1960 Rome Olympics, when he took out the 100 metre freestyle. Not because he was thought to have cheated, per se, but because the race was very (very, very) close.

Actually, you might want to add another 'very' to that sentence, and while you're at, maybe add a few more. As a *New York Times* journalist later put it, the Sydneysider and the American silver medallist, Lance Larson, were 'no further apart than a flattened sardine.' Just a fraction of a second separated the two swimmers at a time when it was up to a panel of judges to decide a race winner, and electronic timers were only used as a backup.

In this case, the decision took almost twenty minutes to arrive. Larson spent most of them posing for photographers and being congratulated by his opponents, while Devitt sat quietly in a sad, lonely corner, after taking a moment to shake the 'winner's hand. 'Personally, I didn't know if I hit first, or not,' the twenty-three-year-old later said.

> There was lots of spray, and it was so fast nobody could tell. What I do remember distinctly is Bob Kiphuth, the legendary swim coach from Yale University, coming across and telling Larson he had won. I had a lot of respect for Kiphuth, so after hearing his verdict I climbed out of the pool and congratulated Larson. I then found out that many other people at the finish and in the stands thought *I* had won and told me so. However, just as many thought Larson had won.

But the decision wasn't up to Kiphuth. It was up to six watching judges.

Who were, of course, evenly split.

The electronic timekeepers, however, were completely unanimous. All six showed Larson as having the faster time of 55.1 seconds, just ahead of Devitt's 55.2. In such cases, the protocol was clear. Defer to the stopwatches, raise the US flag and start playing 'The Star-Spangled Banner'.

But, for some reason, the chief judge decided not to do this. Overruling all six timekeepers and three of his five fellow judges, he simply took 0.1 seconds off Larson's official time and awarded his rival a shiny gold medal. 'If the judges change their placings, I am perfectly willing to give the medal back,' Devitt later said, when the US team launched an (unsuccessful) appeal. 'I have always been taught to accept the judges' decision.'

'Snowy' Baker, on the other hand, was slightly less willing to accept the judge's decision that saw him miss out on a gold at the 1908 London Olympics. Once described as 'the greatest sporting all-rounder [that our nation has] ever produced', the blonde-haired Sydneysider represented Australia in rugby union, swimming, diving and polo, and played cricket at a very high level. But while he was also 'proficient in surfing, fencing, hockey, rowing, yachting and equestrian events,' the 70 kilogram stripling was above all a boxer – and a boxer who was good enough to become Australia's heavyweight champion at the slim, pimply age of eighteen.

But Baker never, alas, became an *Olympic* boxing champion, despite putting up a hell of a show. Competing in the middleweight division,

Baker won three fights in the course of a day on his way to a gold medal match in the evening – a match in which his opponent was England's own Johnny Douglas Jr. Douglas Jr was a boxer who for some reason had only had to fight twice before getting a place in the final. And a boxer whose father happened to the president of the Amateur Boxing Association, the organisation that was running the tournament.

'One of the most brilliant exhibitions of skilful boxing ... ever seen,' the fight that followed was 'a desperately close thing'. In fact, it was so close that it actually split the judges, according to one Snowy Baker. As he told the story – pretty much nonstop, for decades –this 'split decision' was only resolved when an administrator stepped in and decided to present Johnny Douglas Jr with the gold. That administrator's name, it may not surprise you to hear, was of course John Douglas Sr.

Another sporting official to raise a few eyebrows that decade was a Melbournian named 'Mr Allen'. An umpire in the Victorian Football Association – a league that contributed eleven clubs to what we now call the AFL – Allen's first name has been lost to history. But Richmond fans probably knew him as 'Dick'.

It's said this Allen made enemies in Tigerland back in 1904 while umpiring a game Richmond lost to North Melbourne. North Melbourne are now called 'the Kangaroos', but back then they were known as 'the Shinboners', possibly because of a penchant for violence. In any case, it's said that the first half of the match involved a lot of 'rough play' and 'persistent time-wasting' from their players, which

Mr Allen conspicuously failed to control. What was worse, as far as Richmond was concerned, was that a lot of these Shinboners seemed to be wearing long, sharp (and highly illegal) iron spikes on their boots and using them to kick, scratch and stomp.

At half-time, therefore, Richmond officials approached Allen with the request that he inspect said boots. Allen asked the North Melbourne captain if that would be okay – and was promptly informed that no, it was not. Some umpires might treat such an answer as suspicious. This one just shrugged his shoulders instead and proceeded to preside over two more quarters of bloodshed.

The North Melbourne captain was subsequently reprimanded by the VFA – but, for whatever reason, Allen received a promotion. He was formally appointed umpire for the 1904 Grand Final. A Grand Final that, as fate would have it, was due to be played between Richmond and North.

Richmond, which had finished the regular season at the top of the ladder, did not seem to take the news terribly well. You could tell this from the way it immediately asked the VFA to appoint someone else. And from the way it chose to forfeit the Grand Final when that request was refused, and hand North Melbourne the 1904 Premiership, which the Shinboners still prize to this day.

But if we were awarding trophies for dodgy premierships, it would have to go to the South Sydney Rabbitohs. Way back in 1909, when the NRL was the NSW Rugby League, it was proposed that that season's Grand Final be played as the curtain-raiser to an exhibition match between the Wallabies and the Kangaroos that had long been scheduled for later that day. Both the Rabbitohs and Balmain objected to the idea, largely because an earlier kick-off meant that many of their players would still be at work.

The league, however, was inflexible. So the two teams agreed to forfeit the final.

But one of them actually didn't.

'It should be taken away,' said Balmain great Benny Elias about the premierships that South Sydney instantly won when they turned up on time, unopposed.

> People take gold medals away from Olympians who cheat. I would say this is on par. It's clearly stated in the records that they both agreed not to turn up. One team did, and they won the premiership. They weren't honourable in our agreement. We were outsmarted. It was very cunning.

The good news, I suppose, after all these tainted wins, is that not a single person begrudges Steven Bradbury. The poster boy for lucky sportspeople all over the world, this so-so speedskater became the second Australian ever to win a gold medal at the Winter Olympics, thanks to three consecutive flukes in 2002.

Fluke number one came after Bradbury was knocked out in the quarterfinals. A result that, while disappointing, was far from a surprise, given that by then, he was well past his best. After sliding in the rankings for close to a decade, the twenty-nine-year-old had recently broken his neck and been bedridden for months. A quarterfinal appearance was pretty good going, in the circumstances. For that matter, so was being able to walk.

Only it turned out he couldn't just walk off into retirement. Because one of the other quarterfinalists was disqualified for pushing. Our hero suddenly found himself having to race in the semis.

Which brings us to fluke number two. Also carrying scars from another accident that saw him lose six litres of blood, Bradbury was doing his manful best in a star-studded race. Which of course meant that he was coming dead last. Younger, fitter and infinitely faster, his highly ranked rivals were all bunched together, far, far ahead of him.

But there was an upside to this slightly embarrassing state of affairs, one that came when one of his rivals went down. Because when that rival tripped over, all the others did too. Right into a tangled, bloody heap on the ice. Lagging far behind the pack as he was, Bradbury had plenty of room to weave his way past all the chaos, and waltz home for a cheeky win.

For fluke number three, please repeat fluke number two. Only replace the word 'semifinal' with the word 'final'. And throw in a gold medal too.

'Yeah, it was an insane moment,' says the first-ever man to 'do a Bradbury'.

> One of the most memorable moments in the history of sport, and I was fortunate to be there at the right place at the right time. I wasn't sure if

I should put my arms out in the air and celebrate or if I should quickly go and hide in the corner. I didn't really know what the appropriate response was at that moment. Even afterwards, I was sitting in the change rooms – and obviously the look on my face as I went across the finish line tells most of the story, one of disbelief – but I had a few moments before I had to go to the medal ceremony and the media conference and when I was in the change room I wasn't sure if I was going to either of them because I didn't know if I wanted to accept the gold medal under those circumstances but after a few minutes I decided yeah I'll go out on the podium, and I'll accept this gold medal. But not for the 90 seconds of the race – I'm going to take it for the 14 years of hard work, five hours a day, six days a week for 14 years.

That's not that lucky. I think I'll take it for that.

The Luck of the Devil

Aussies who got away with murder

'I broke a mirror in my house. I'm supposed to get seven years of bad luck, but my lawyer thinks he can get me five.'
Steven Wright, US comedian

How did human beings become so smart?

Part of the answer may be through our jaws. About 2.4 million years ago (give or take a few weeks), a random African primate was born with usually small jaw muscles and a desire to make the beast with two backs. By shagging around, they spread it around – a development that, in the short-term, might not have looked much like good luck. But in the long-term, I think we can probably say that it was. Because it gave our brains room to more than triple in size.

Of course, not every brain necessarily falls into this category. Take the one belonging to Tony Prince. 'We didn't really want to rob a bank,' recalls that Byron Bay bad boy, of the time he and a friend decided to rob a bank. 'We were just talking about it and thinking about it and joking about how we could actually do it and then before we knew it, it just turned serious.'

Based in a small Colorado ski town during a 2005 working holiday, the neuron-light teenagers thought long and hard about which bank to target. Eventually they decided to rob the one bank at which they were both regular customers. Because it was right next door to the shop where they worked.

In fairness, they were at least clever enough to arm themselves with fake guns and cover their faces with black masks. But they were not quite clever enough to try to hide their broad Australian accents. Or to remove the big tags they wore at the store ... which told the world they were 'Tony' and 'Luke'.

'I would say we had them identified within eight minutes of the robbery,' says a local detective of the pair, who seem to have spent their brief getaway buying Rolex watches and two one-way tickets to Mexico. They were also careful to tip the local cabbie $20,000 when he took them to the airport, and to take photos of each other holding big wads of cash, which they then helpfully saved on their phones.

Unfortunately for police, however, not every criminal is that easy to catch. For every ten chumps who may as well march into a courtroom chanting 'I did it', there are plenty of crims who manage to avoid getting convicted. And plenty of them owe their freedom to luck.

Take the person who raped and killed twelve-year-old redhead Alma Tirtschke in a dark Melbourne lane in 1921. We don't know who he was, but we know who he *wasn't*: Colin Ross, the man hanged for her murder. The owner of a shop not far from the lane where the unfortunate girl met her grim end, Ross was a perfectly reputable citizen, and one who was perfectly able to account for his movements. But he wasn't able to account for the strands of red hair that police found on his person. Strands of red hair that got him convicted. And that modern DNA tests show did not come from Alma.

In a forensically researched book that led to Ross's exoneration (several decades after he was, alas, hanged), Kevin Morgan suggests that the real culprit was most likely Alma's creepy cousin, a traumatised WWI veteran with 'paedophilic tendencies'. But the bottom line is that we'll probably never know whodunnit. Just as we'll probably never know the real names of Jack the Ripper, Bible John, the Zodiac Killer, Mr Cruel or the Monster of Florence.

Other times, however, police *do* know whodunnit; they just can't get quite enough evidence to secure a conviction. Take Thomas Turner, for example, the man who was quite clearly the brains behind Australia's first bank robbery. A convict who became a stonemason in the 1820s, he was hired by the Bank of Australia's Sydney headquarters to convert its basement into a safe. After a few days of digging and chiselling and chipping and so on, Turner discovered that this basement was directly above a sewerage pipe. A sewerage pipe that was big enough for someone to crawl through. And a sewerage pipe that could be accessed from outside.

And a sewerage pipe that was shortly afterwards accessed in just such a way, by a handful of guys who Tom happened to know.

We know who they were, because – seeking to shorten his sentence for another crime, later on – one of them was eventually moved to confess. But while William Blackstone cheerfully ratted on four of his colleagues, he refused to confirm Turner's role in the haul because, by all accounts, the pair were good chums. Turner remained a 'person of interest' for the rest of his conspicuously affluent life, and a frequent target of police raids, but no admissible evidence was ever found.

Another person that the police got to know pretty well over the years was a young sex worker from London named Tilly Devine. Arriving in Sydney in 1920, after marrying an Aussie soldier during the war, the 'vivacious, pretty and streetwise' Devine managed to get arrested at least seventy-nine times for doing an honest night's work. Generally, an arrest just meant a night in the clink, but when she was sentenced to two years' hard labour in 1925, the notorious sex worker began to wonder if some kind of career change might not be an idea.

So she became a notorious madam instead, going on to open several popular, prosperous, action-packed brothels in and around Woolloomooloo. Permanently clad in diamonds and furs, Tilly may have been 'a vicious, grasping, high-priestess of savagery, venery, obscenity and whoredom' (to quote her less-than-glowing 1970 obituary), but she was also a perfectly legitimate businessperson, thanks to a lucky loophole in NSW law.

The *Police Offences (Amendment) Act* 1908 had made it an offence for a man to operate a brothel, act as a pimp or profit from the earnings of prostitution. But never said anything at all about a woman ...

Another lucky woman when it came to legal fine print was a Melbourne mother named Gordana Parezanovic. In 2002 she attempted to do what common sense would really suggest a young mother should not: secrete a heap of heroin into the folds of her clothes and get on a plane to Malaysia. Malaysia being a country where drug smugglers get the death sentence. A mandatary death sentence, with zero exceptions. No matter which country a person might hail from.

So, there was no reason to imagine that Parezanovic was about to have a good day when staff at Kuala Lumpur International Airport ordered her to step aside and be searched. 'With that amount she wouldn't have stood a ghost of a chance,' said her lawyer, Karpal Singh, of the 3 kilograms of a 'chocolate-coloured substance' that said searchers were quick to discover.

But the big question, for Singh, was *where* they discovered it. Technically speaking, you see, Gordana had been standing in a transit lounge at the time of her search and arrest. Which, technically speaking, meant that she had not actually been standing in the country of Malaysia. And so did not actually bring drugs inside it.

Thanks to this technicality, Gordana got away with five years in jail. She's probably still shaking with sweet, sweet relief.

Rather less lucky when it came to their sentence were the Sydney-and-Brisbane-based Bali Nine. Convicted of trying to smuggle

8.3 kilograms of heroin out of Indonesia, way back in 2005, most of the Bali Nine are still stuck in prison and will probably remain there for life.

The two ringleaders, however, have no life left, after being put in front of a firing squad in 2015. But *were* Andrew Chan and Myuran Sukumaran the actual ringleaders? Or were they in fact just a couple of low-level couriers – just a couple of humble mules for a major drug ring? Chan, it's worth noting, was just twenty-one at the time of his arrest, while Sukumaran was a mere twenty-five. Most of us would struggle to organise a fridge at that age, let alone run a major crime ring. Neither man had a criminal record, or a particularly lavish lifestyle. Both had crappy jobs, and Chan lived with his parents.

According to multiple news reports, police believe that the Nine's actual 'mastermind' is a notorious Sydney man who managed to get off scot-free because he did all his masterminding well away from Indonesia. The subject of numerous criminal investigations, because of his suspected role at the head of a syndicate, the man was never named in court by either Chan or Sukumaran, with both defendants 'citing fears for the safety of their families'. He was said to be living an 'extravagant' 'life of luxury' back home in Sydney, right around the time they were sentenced to death.

This in and of itself seems pretty lucky for him. But his run of good fortune certainly didn't stop there. According to the *Sydney Morning Herald*, the year of the trial also saw the alleged mastermind buy a lottery ticket ... turn on the telly ... and discover that he had just won a tidy $5 million.

As *SMH* journo Michael Bachelard put it, 'The extraordinary luck of the man underlines the rarely spoken reality of drug busts: those arrested are usually mid- to low-level players. More senior syndicate members ensure they are not hands-on and continue to traffic drugs once a courier or shore-party is arrested.'

But it's not only drug lords who get away with murder. Supermodels sometimes can and do too. A semifinalist in the Miss Australia pageant, and occasional cover model for Pix, the twenty-one-year-old 'blonde, attractive' Shirley Beiger became a successful figure in the Sydney fashion scene after leaving school in the late 1940s. Her personal life seemed to be going well, too, when she hooked up with a certain Arthur Griffith, a 'handsome, clean cut' twenty-three-year-old clerk, who newspapers also described as a 'keen sports player' and 'regular nightclub habitue'.

By 9 August 1953, however, Griffith's regular habit appeared to have got out of hand. Convinced that her lover was having an affair, Beiger decided to follow him to his late-night 'dental appointment' and discovered that he had, in fact, gone to a nightclub 'with a girl on his arm'.

I would like to report that the drama ended then and there, and she drove home to pack her bags. But, while Beiger did indeed drive home, she did so to fetch a rifle, and before long she was back at the club. Her plan, she later told a jury, had been to 'tell him if he didn't come home with me, I would shoot myself'.

But like so many good plans, this one went awry. The reason being that she shot him instead.

Held the following November, Beiger's murder trial was a media sensation, attracting 'day long queue[s] of sensation-seekers, armed with cut lunches and refreshments'. When Beiger was finally called to the witness box, she accordingly put on a show 'answering questions in a soft, almost inaudible voice – a speech stifled by sobs and great emotional strain'. Shortly before being assisted from the witness box, angelic face covered with soft, dewy tears, our heroine insisted that she hadn't meant for the gun to go off, and that it had only done so because Griffith gave her a 'push'. 'I was holding something with my right hand. I didn't know at the time what it was ... I didn't realise what had happened.'

The media responded with appropriate scepticism. 'Beiger appeared in court wearing a fashionable slate-grey gabardine tent coat buttoned right to the neck,' noted one hardened journo, while others savaged the way her 'corn-coloured hair was cut in the latest "poodle"' or attacked her 'wide-brimmed hat, and yellow gloves'.

The Truth was even more ruthless. 'The blonde, carefree beauty with the teasing smile, the bright chatter is no longer,' it wrote. 'In her place is a girl with sombre eyes and a lip that trembles.'

In his summing up, the all-male judge reminded the all-male jury that, 'There is no such thing as a crime of passion in our jurisprudence.' Just because Beiger was a 'not unattractive young woman', they should not be 'swayed by motives of compassion'. If they thought that Griffith's death was intended, then their verdict must be murder. And if they thought that Beiger's gun went off by accident, they should at least bring in a verdict of involuntary manslaughter.

So, murder or manslaughter. What was it to be?

The answer, of course, was neither.

When the jury declared the defendant 'not guilty', '150 members of the public in court cheered and clapped wildly for two minutes'. The hundreds gathered outside quickly joined in the cheers, while many more sent her flowers, chocolates and congratulatory telegrams, or lapped up her story when it was serialised in the *Sun*. Refusing all requests for an interview, Beiger went on to live a quiet life in Melbourne, well away from the public eye (and, one would hope, any rifles).

But the consequences of 'getting away with it' can sometimes be a little more serious. Take, for example, a seventeen-year-old psychopath from suburban Sydney who took a taxi in 1962. Prone to 'anti-social behaviour', such as cutting dogs in half with a machete, this car-stealing, housebreaking school dropout had only just been released from a juvenile detention centre. His next stop, you would think, would be jail. 'He was going to kill somebody from the age of 10,' his brother fondly recalled years later. 'It was built into him ... I knew he was on a one-way trip. I knew that it was just a matter of how long.'

In all fairness, however, our 'gun crazy' hero didn't kill anyone that day. All he did was shoot the taxi driver in the spine, for no apparent reason, rendering him a paraplegic for the rest of his days.

But said teenager didn't go to jail for this crime. In fact, he never even spoke to police. Reason being, they thought 'another young petty criminal' was to blame – a man who wrongly believed that his young brother was responsible, and so nobly 'confessed' to protect him.

A false confession that meant that that young petty criminal spent years behind bars, while ours wandered free and made a name for himself.

That name was Ivan Milat.

Lucky in Love

How a 'floating brothel' actually helped to save lives

> 'I've had bad luck with both my wives. The first one left me and the second one didn't.'
>
> Patrick Murray, English actor

True beauty, they say, tends to lie on the inside: in who you are rather than how you appear. In order to look good, you just have to *do* good, and so on, and so on, and so forth.

Unfortunately, 'they' are full of it. True beauty, I'm sad to report, tends to lie in straight teeth, evenly spaced eyes and a symmetrical jaw. Throw in high cheekbones, full lips and thick hair, and it really doesn't matter if you are ugly on the inside – if, beneath your smooth skin, there lies a foul core. You're still going to be a looker. A hottie. Babelicious. A stud. A stone-cold fox and/or a perfect ten.

But are you going to be lucky in love? Some academics seem to have a few doubts. While studies have shown that being hot can be a help in the workplace, it may be less of an asset when it comes to relationships. Or, in fact, not an asset at all.

A Harvard team recently went through thousands of old high school yearbooks, rated each student's physical attractiveness, then researched their later lives on Ancestry.com. They found that the hot ones were 'overwhelmingly' more likely to have never been married, or to have gone through at least one divorce.

The reason, they concluded, may actually be this very hotness, simply because it makes getting sex so much easier. Whether or not they actually cheat on their partner, a hot person will always feel like they *could*. Every time they exchange a glance with a workmate, or a laugh with a stranger, a part of them will feel like the opportunity for a shag is right there in front of them; that alternative partners are lying thick on the ground.

'Big deal,' you say? Well, you're right. It sure is. Because just as it can be hard to be completely satisfied with, say, a burger when you're in a food court filled with sushi and Thai, 'having too many other choices is likely not beneficial for relationship longevity'. Excessive choice is relationship cancer – and breaking up is the easiest cure. Why put the work into a long-term relationship when you can just go up to the counter and eat something else?

Why? Why? I'll tell you why. Because a good relationship is actually quite hard to find. If your working assumption is that each of us has a soulmate – one special person out there who it is our life's task to find – then the odds of finding them are really quite dreadful. You are, after all, living in a world of eight billion people. Most of them speaking languages that you don't understand and living in places that you'll never go.

But there are times, of course, when we don't need a soulmate – when we don't need to find the missing piece of life's puzzle; when we don't need the warmth of love's flame.

Often this is because there's good stuff on Netflix.

But other times, it's because we just want a shag.

So, I'd ask you spare a thought for Australia's first straight, male settlers – a group for whom the pickings were slim. And when I say slim, I mean flat-out skeletal. Australia's male to female ratio is pretty much even Stevens today (or, if you prefer, all-square Claire). But up until the 1830s, the colony was basically one big sausagefest: we had roughly six men for every one woman.

If you think that this sounds like a recipe for a lot of male bonding, one suspects that you would be correct. 'What will ensue when we have thousands of men cooped up in the colony without wives and unable to seek them elsewhere?' asked one prison chaplain. 'Evil,' he answered, 'will be the result.' An evil 'too humiliating for the mind to dwell upon.' An evil 'too revolting to name.'

How could a God-fearing government possibly combat such wickedness? Clearly by sending more chicks. A sort of 'unofficial breeding program for the colony,' the *Lady Juliana* was a 401-ton barque sent in 1789 with only lady convicts aboard. Most of them 'fresh (and) well looking' sex workers aged in their 20s and 30s.

With the *Juliana*'s thirty-seven officers all encouraged to take on a 'wife', no less than thirty-seven children were born during the curiously slow voyage. A voyage that ended up taking about twice as long as planned, due to a few leisurely stops in the tropics.

But for all that the power balance in these 'marriages' might have been a bit iffy, and likely to be frowned upon by the folks in HR, 'the floating brothel' may not have just been good luck for all the people with penises. It may have a been a stroke of luck for the women as well.

Penny Edwell is just one of many historians to write that the women 'were not coerced', while Libby-Jane Charleston goes so far as to say that the 320-day sex-fest 'worked out rather splendidly for all.'

The ship was kept clean. They could wear their own clothes. There was no question of locks or chains. All were allowed up on deck, to do what they like (or, indeed, who), and the records suggest that the rations were generous.

> 'It didn't really matter if the couples came together due to lust, love or basic necessity ... [these "marriages"] made life onboard a lot easier and certainly a lot less lonely.' All in all, their experience was 'clearly pleasurable, compared to the experience of the First Fleet and sheer heaven compared to the hell that was the Second Fleet [which saw more than 40 per cent of those aboard die].'

And 'not only were the women allowed many exclusive privileges,' Charleston writes, 'they were also given the opportunity to greatly improve their position – not only on the ship but for their future, as many of these ship love affairs were long lasting.'

It's certainly true that all aboard arrived in Sydney in usually good health, and went on to live long, full and prosperous lives.

Relationship perfection? Clearly not. But it's important to remember that the alternative was London's prisons. Dark, rancid dungeons where the next stop was death. Either from the noose or some noxious disease.

And even if they somehow managed to get out of jail alive, it wouldn't have been long before they were back, because these were people with zero prospects. Not so much second-class citizens, as in a social category just below pond scum, poor London women didn't *have* to steal or do sex work during the late 18th century. But they did if they wanted to eat.

But on the 'love boat', they didn't just get freedom, food, sunshine and fresh air. Some may have even found love. Take this touching diary extract from John Nicol, the *Lady Juliana*'s Scottish steward, about his onboard 'wife', Sarah Whitlam.

> She was a native of Lincoln, a girl of modest reserved turn, as kind and true a creature as ever lived. I courted her for a week and upwards, and would have married her upon the spot, had there been a clergy man on board ... I had fixed my fancy upon her from the moment I knocked the

rivet out of her irons upon my anvil, and as firmly resolved to bring her back to England, when her time was out, my lawful wife, as ever I did intend anything in my life.

Sadly, Sarah left him for somebody else. True soulmates are quite hard to find.

Beginner's Luck

Australian actors who got lucky breaks

> 'No one knows the life-changing power of luck better than actors. Just the sheer odds of standing out among thousands of bright-faced, oh-so-impossibly attractive aspiring actors could test the stamina of a Zen master.'
>
> Jay Williams, US writer

There's no business like show business – if your goal is to get low self-esteem. A recent survey by a London university suggested that only 2 per cent of actors actually make a living from the stage or the screen. To be an actor is essentially to be a waiter or a cleaner or an Uber driver. But a waiter/cleaner/Uber driver who also has to spend their time auditioning for parts ... and getting rejected pretty much every time. To be an actor is to hope against hope, and then have that hope crushed. Then repeat the process, day in, day out, year in and year out, until you lose your will to live. Or at least until the hope is all gone.

And LA, of course, is even worse, that city being a sort of magnet for actors. Go there and you won't just see traffic and smog and billboards and cement and Latino workers being paid next to nothing. You will see hordes and hordes and hordes of hotties. Endless roomfuls of charismatic, well-spoken, outgoing sex gods with gleaming white teeth and rich golden tan. They go to every audition. They attend every party. They schmooze with producers twenty-four hours a day. Every single one of them will tell you that they're 'passionate' about acting – then produce a headshot and demo reel to prove it. In a universe this big, it's hard to be a star. You need a little bit of luck to stand out from the pack.

Or maybe you just need a punch in the face. Mel Gibson, for example, has an extremely punchable face, and I'm not just saying that because of his shit personality. Legend has it that the once-obscure NIDA graduate didn't even *mean* to audition for the role of 'Mad Max', the battered, vengeful cop in the 1979 film that went on to make him a star. He just happened to be driving a friend to the audition. What's more, he just happened to be driving him after a 'very bad weekend,' which had involved a fairly massive pub brawl. 'I didn't come out looking too pretty,' the recovering alcoholic recalls. 'I took on half a rugby team and ... it didn't work out too well on my end. So I was looking pretty bad [while I] waited for [my friend] in the waiting room with the girls at the casting agency.'

But it turned out that – making the violent film that they were – this sort of violent look was just what they wanted. 'They took polaroids because I was – really – every colour of the rainbow, and they put them up, and they said: "Man, we need freaks in this film! When you heal up come and see us."' So he did. And a star was soon born.

Simon Baker has a similar story. Most famous these days for his starring role in *The Mentalist*, the Tassie boy was also just driving a friend to an audition (for an ad) when he was asked to read a few lines himself. Working as a pool attendant at a Gold Coast resort, he had never acted before that day. But he has never stopped since.

Naomi Watts, the blonde Aussie star of *King Kong*, also got her big break when accompanying a friend. In 1991, a pal of the then-twenty-year-old drama student managed to wangle a couple of tickets to the premiere of *Dead Calm*. 'I met the director, John Duigan, there. He said, "I'm doing a movie, *Flirting*, and you look like the perfect type for it. Would you call the casting director and maybe we can read with you?" So I did, and I got the part.'

Olivia Newton-John was equally lucky in her choice of pals, way back in 1977. A moderately successful country music singer who made occasional forays into pop, Newton-John had appeared in an ill-fated 'science fiction musical' in 1970, and had wisely avoided acting ever since. The twenty-nine-year-old did not, however, avoid a dinner with Helen Reddy, another Melbourne-born singer, when they both happened to be in London at the same time.

And a good thing, too, because the dinner also happened to be attended by Allan Carr, a fairly obscure Hollywood producer who'd just bought the film rights to a fairly obscure off-Broadway musical about a bunch of Chicago high schoolers back in the 50s. Olivia may have been almost thirty. She may have been an Aussie. She may have had the acting skills of a spatula. But she also had a certain something – a sort of sweet, wholesome chasteness – that made Carr say, 'You're the one that I want.'

Errol Flynn also had no intentions of being an actor when he was in his twenties. The Tasmanian school dropout just wanted to be paid to captain boats in and around Papua New Guinea (a place where he also smuggled the occasional diamond and found a lot of work as a gigolo). But in 1933, one of the people paying Errol to sail a boat just happened to be a film producer who was making a movie about the mutiny on the *Bounty*. A movie whose main character was a dashingly handsome sailor with leadership skills, and a rebellious streak. Errol essentially didn't have to 'act' at all. (And some might say that he never actually did.)

Cate Blanchett also didn't need to act to get her big break, though the fact that she could meant that she sure made the most of it. In 1995, an arthouse director named Shekhar Kapur was recruited by a major studio to make a film about Elizabeth I. He had a great script. He had a big budget. And he had a near-complete cast and crew. But as 1995 turned into 1996, and started to creep towards 1997, he also had a problem. He still didn't have an actor who could serve as Elizabeth. Madonna and Bette Midler had both been suggested by a studio keen on a big name, along with the fast-rising Kate Winslet.

But Kapur held out for someone special – until one day he found her, when a trailer for an obscure Australian movie happened to appear on the telly. Needless to say, it starred the equally obscure Cate Blanchett, a twenty-eight-year-old NIDA graduate who had yet to work a day overseas.

'The moment I saw her, I knew I had found my perfect Elizabeth,' said Kapur. 'I wanted to make a contemporary film that is also historical and Cate has an amazing face, it's almost translucent. You don't quite know what age it belongs to. It belongs to then, it belongs to now. Her beauty is regal.'

Hugh Jackman's beauty, on the other hand, almost cost him the role that more or less made his movie career. 'He was great, but he was the nicest guy in the world and he was very tall and super handsome, so we didn't think he was Wolverine,' says the casting director of the first *X-Men* movie. He auditioned the 6 foot 3 inch Australian actor seven times, before going on to cast Dougray Scott as the irascible, hairy comic-book mutant, who's supposed to be 5 foot three inches.

At the time, Jackman was getting plenty of theatre work. And chances are he would have continued to tread the boards for the rest of his days, had the production of *Mission: Impossible 2* run according to schedule. Dougray Scott, you see, also got a part in that film, which was supposed to have wrapped before *X-Men* got shooting. But as luck would have it, it ran overtime – and its producer (a man by the name of Tom Cruise) refused to let him work on both films.

'He was like, "You've got to stay and finish the film" and I said I will, but I'll go and do that as well,' Scott recalled. 'For whatever reason he said I couldn't. He was a very powerful guy. Other people were doing everything to make it work.'

With their Wolverine stuck in an ironclad contract and shooting due to start within days, *X-Men*'s producers desperately turned to an Australian alternative. By which I of course mean Russell Crowe. But Crowe turned down the offer and suggested a friend instead. A friend who had already auditioned for the role, and who went on to play it nine times.

Hugh is now said to be worth about US$180 million.

There's no business like show business, if your goal is to get wealth and fame.

PART FOUR

A FIGHTING CHANCE

Have you ever wondered how Michael Jordan became such a great basketballer? Or how Serena Williams managed to win all those Grand Slams, and Tiger Woods got so very good at golf?

Well, there's innate talent, of course. And lots of hard work. Plus a sort of deranged single-mindedness and competitive spirit that they should probably try to unpack with a therapist. (It's generally something to do with your parents.)

But if you can put all of that stuff aside for a minute, the answer might just be lucky charms. Jordan, you see, always wore the same old 'lucky' pair of shorts from back in his college days, underneath his official team clothes. Serena, for her part, would always stick with the same pair of socks as she made her way through a tournament, while Woods would always pop on a lucky red shirt when he needed to come home strong during a big final round.

Well, so what, you say. What does that prove? Apart from the fact they were all superstitious (and hopefully fans of deodorant)?

Well, it's possible that these charms actually prove quite a lot, when you consider the success of their owners. Because study after study has tended to suggest that believing in luck is a self-fulfilling prophecy. That people are generally more likely to win if they believe that they have luck on their side. A 2010 study, for example, 'found that golfers who were told they were using a "lucky ball" performed better than those who were not'.

Call it the power of positive thinking or, if you prefer, the placebo effect. The basic point is that life is filled with all sorts of tough battles – all sorts of fights that seem to promise defeat. But an extra dollop of confidence, however dubious its source, can often be all we need to actually chalk up the win.

That said, I brought a lucky charm to golf the other day and somehow managed to reach a whole new level of shit. A level of sheer wanton dreadfulness that it would only be possible to surpass if I was to surgically remove both of my arms.

So sometimes, I guess, actual luck is required if you are to have, yes, a fighting chance.

Soldiers of Fortune

WWI veterans who dodged a bullet

'Every soldier owes the fact that he is still alive to a thousand lucky chances and nothing else. And every soldier believes in and trusts to chance.'

Erich Maria Remarque, *All Quiet on the Western Front*

It's often said – to me, at least – that being a writer is a waste of a life. That to sit alone and silent, day after day, is to squander the precious gift of existence. We should be mingling. Getting out and about. Interacting with our fellow man.

As someone who has met my fellow man, however, this is an idea that I tend to reject. On the whole, they are pretty hard work.

WWI, on the other hand, was most definitely a waste of a life. Or, more to the point, it was a waste of about 22 million lives – 60,000 of them, of course, Australian. 'Futile', 'senseless', 'utterly pointless' and 'the worst act of political malpractice in history', it was a famously avoidable fight about nothing. A diplomatic spat that snowballed out of control.

What happened, in short, was that European diplomats had spent the hundred-or-so years since the Napoleonic Wars forming various alliances. Come 1914, this meant that pretty much every country had promised themselves to at least one other nation if they got tangled up in a war, provided that said nation would also help them. 'Europe was tinderbox waiting for a spark.'

And that spark of course came in 1914, when the heir to the Austro-Hungarian throne, Archduke Franz Ferdinand, was assassinated in his car during a visit to Sarajevo.

Why? Well, the assassination led Austria-Hungary to declare war on Serbia.

Which meant that Serbia's ally, Russia, had to declare war on Austria-Hungary.

Which meant that Austria-Hungary's ally, Germany, had to declare war on Russia.

Which meant that Russia's ally, France, had to declare war on Germany.

Which meant that France's ally, England, had to declare war as well.

Which meant that poor old Australia had to come along, too.

Given the scale of the slaughter that followed, Franz Ferdinand's assassination is seen as one of the most pivotal moments in all human history. It was a rock in the pond of international affairs whose ripples are being felt to this day.

And here's the thing: it was all down to bad luck. Franz Ferdinand should have been perfectly fine.

His assassins, after all, were not exactly Jason Bourne. Calling themselves the Black Hand, maybe because Red Face was already taken, we're talking about seven pimply students who had never even picked up a gun, let alone actually shot one in anger. But being determined to strike a glorious blow against the Austro-Hungarian empire (and, who knows, maybe impress a few girls), they quietly joined the crowds that were lining the streets to greet the archduke, guns and grenades tucked away in their pockets. They were armed and ready.

No, scratch that. They were just armed. Six of the seven students 'simply froze with terror as the [archduke's motorcade] approached', says Cambridge historian Christopher Clark. 'They were scarcely more than boys, really. Very inexperienced.'

One of them, however, was made of sterner stuff. Despite the presence of police, and total impossibility of escape, Nedeljko Čabrinović finally managed to screw up his courage when Franz's car passed and hurl his grenade straight at its boot. The good news was that he got a direct hit. The bad news was that the grenade had a ten-second fuse. This meant that it simply bounced off the car and rolled under the one travelling behind it, mildly injuring a minor official.

Franz's car naturally sped off after seeing the blast, and even more naturally, so too did Nedeljko. Taking a swig from a vial of cyanide that he'd keep under his coat, the teenager raced through the crowds, then hurled himself off a ledge and into a river to drown.

Whereupon he discovered the even worse news. His cyanide was harmless, having expired long ago. And the river was four inches deep.

Seeing Nedeljko get arrested as he lay in a puddle, clutching a broken leg, five other members of the Black Hand quickly sprang into action. By which I mean that they all ran away.

The one exception was Gavrilo Princip, a pale, 'small and weak' nineteen-year-old with an extremely bad case of tuberculosis. He seems to have decided to go get a snack. And it was while Gavrilo was standing outside Schiller's Delicatessen on Franz Joseph Street a little while later that something really quite strange occurred.

Franz, you see, had not immediately rushed back to Vienna, as his entourage had strongly advised. He had attended a reception at City Hall. After that was over, he decided to make one alteration to his otherwise carefully planned schedule – spontaneously ordering his chauffeur to drive he and his wife to the local hospital, in their open-top convertible, so they could visit the injured official.

It would have been a lovely gesture, had the chauffeur known where the local hospital was. But being from out of town, he did not. Which inevitably meant that he made a wrong turn ... right onto Franz Joseph Street. When the driver realised his mistake, he slowed to a halt ... right outside Schiller's Delicatessen ... and then discovered that the engine was stalled.

All of which was news for a wan, sickly weed who just happened to be standing about four feet away. Not one to shun a gift from the gods, Gavrilo Princip slowly pulled out his gun ... aimed it right at the duke ... and completely missed, accidentally killing his wife. But he still had plenty of time to shoot again. And with this second shot, he finally succeeded in killing his man. And in so doing managed to kickstart a chain of events that led to the worst war in history.

Now, I'm conscious that, as strokes of luck go, this one wasn't great, unless your name happened to be Gavrilo. It certainly wasn't great for the 60,000 Australian soldiers who enlisted to fight, and whose bodies never made it back home. Most of them still lie in Gallipoli, Greece, Belgium or France. Or Egypt or Syria or Lebanon.

But we can count ourselves lucky, in a sense, that many *did* make it home. Without the occasional flash of good fortune, Australia's death toll could have been even worse.

Take Private Griffith Owen, for example: a Fremantle greengrocer and keen lawn bowler who lived to a robust old age. One of the first Australians to enlist, he really should have become one of the first Australians to die when he landed at Gallipoli in 1915. 'We had only been two hours in the line, where I was placed behind a parapet of sandbags, when suddenly I was staggered by the force of a bullet against my body,' Owen wrote in a letter home.

> I recovered quickly and to my surprise did not feel any pain or observe any blood marks. I had been shot all right, for further search revealed to my astonishment that a bullet had penetrated my greatcoat through my equipment and then into my tunic pocket, inside of which I had a

wallet containing a Testament, and inside that again a little book, in the centre of which the bullet had lodged.

Praise the Lord. Though it has to be said that, when it comes to bulletproof shields, Owen's little Bible was not the only good book. Just ask his fellow Gallipoli veteran Ted Matthews, who was clutching a thick leather pocketbook given to him by his mum when he was hit in the chest with a huge piece of shrapnel.

'I had a bruise but that shrapnel could have hit me in the face, anywhere,' the 'knockabout' Sydney carpenter said decades later, shortly before dying in his sleep aged 101. 'It's all a matter of luck. As we used to say, if your name was on it, you'd get it.'

A piece of shrapnel could also have posed problems for a certain Sergeant Ernest Pittard, were it not for a handful of coins. Ordinarily responsible for laying mines, Pittard was one of a few dozen engineers picked to go 'over the top' at the Battle of Messines – a seven-day bloodbath in a grim corner of Belgium that ultimately cost about 50,000 lives. Pittard and his fellow engineers were told that most of them were unlikely to survive – a blow to morale that probably wasn't much helped during their less-than-relaxed five-hour march to the battlefront. 'Fritz did pepper us with all kinds of shells including 20,000 gas shells,' Pittard later wrote, 'and we lost twenty-six men before we even reached our own front line.'

But the fun was only just getting started. It was while sheltering in a foxhole from 'the rattle of 1000 machine guns', wrote Pittard, that 'a piece of shell hit me and sent me spinning'. But the good news was that it didn't hit *him*, so much as some lose change in his chest pocket. He collapsed to the ground but somehow survived.

Eventually making it back to Melbourne (where he undid all his good work for the nation by helping to build lots of banks), Pittard hung onto his lucky coin for the rest of his life. A period that, alas, was not all that long, thanks to the side effects of a severely bruised heart. 'He came home one day, sat down in the chair and died,' said grandson Geoff McLeod.

'Lucky Les' Holden, on the other hand, seemed to have no bruises to speak of after three action-packed years on the front. Flying at a time when planes had only just been invented and may as well have been made out of Play-Doh, WWI pilots were lucky to stay alive even when there *weren't* people shooting them. Some calculations show a pilot was likely to survive only a little over two weeks in battle. Others show it was closer to one week.

But clearly no one told Lucky Les. A 'modest man with a sunny temperament and whimsical humour,' his ability to be shot and not suffer a scratch quickly turned into a thing of legend. A legend that reached its height during the fog-shrouded Battle of Cambrai, when Les flew back to base in a smoky, burning, bullet-riddled wreck no less than twice in two days. 'Every part of it was shot full of holes,' wrote CEW Bean of Holden's plane, 'including [the] petrol-tank, [the] tail-plane, both longerons, and part of the undercarriage, while the elevator control was shot clean away. [It was] clear evidence of the dangers of the work and of his own good luck'.

And it was a legend that somehow managed to grow even greater, when Holden survived a clash with the famous Red Baron. According to the *Australian Dictionary of Biography*, the invincible German fighter ace 'fired at him from below and the bullets ripped up through the floor and tore his leggings'. But our boy still managed to 'nurse his badly damaged machine home', despite 'losing a wing on impact'.

I'm sad to report, however, that Les's luck didn't last. As irony would have it, he died in 1932. As a passenger on a routine plane flight. Which somehow found a way to crash.

But of all 416,000 Australians who enlisted for WWI, I'd say that the luckiest was John Campbell Ross. A Labor political operative, he became Australia's last living WWI soldier in 2007, at the ripe old age of 108. But John wasn't just lucky because he survived the war. He was lucky because he never fought in the first place. Too young to enlist until 1918, he was all trained up and ready to ship out to France right at the moment the Germans surrendered.

He never had to see people murdered in front of him – or take on the grim task for himself. He never had to deal with the blood and the mud and the rats and the lice. He never had to be blinded by the gas and deafened by guns and be traumatised by the sheer human suffering.

And if we're lucky, nor will you or I.

Bombs that Bombed

Aussies who survived a big bang

'Depend on the rabbit's foot if you will, but remember it didn't work for the rabbit.'

RE Shay, US writer

With its spectacular castle and cobblestoned streets, Kokura is a picturesque monument to Japan's past. Far away from the hustle of nearby Hiroshima, this city's million or so residents spend their springs surrounded by cherry blossoms – and get to walk past ancient shrines every day of the week. If you like ornate parks and esteemed 'schools of swordsmanship', you'll love this clean, green oasis on the island of Kyushu. As cities go, it is strangely serene.

What's even stranger, however, is the fact that it stayed every bit as serene throughout the closing stages of WWII. A period that was of course filled with ferocious bombing raids on cities and towns the length and breadth of Japan. It's been estimated that up to 900,000

Japanese civilians were killed by American pilots, and close to 10 million were rendered homeless. We're talking about a humanitarian catastrophe on par with *The Farmer Wants a Wife*.

'Everybody was kind of wondering why Kokura wasn't bombed, even though we had a big military factory,' recalled one resident, Mutsuharu Odawara. 'Lots of people wondered.'

The answer, we now know, was actually *because* Kokura had a big military factory. Aware that the little town was actually bulging with armaments, the United States very much had Kokura on its hit list. But they were planning to hit it with something quite special. With a brand- new kind of bomb whose brand-new effects they were keen to observe with precision. So they decided to keep Kokura pristine. Until the time came to make it a memory.

That time could well have come on 6 August 1945 – the day that the first nuke famously dropped from the skies, wiping out more than 140,000 people. Kokura was second on America's list of potential targets. Hiroshima was, of course, number one.

Three days later, Japan still hadn't surrendered, so the US decided to drop bomb number two. And after its weather reconnaissance planes reported a clear blue sky over Kokura, that little city was confirmed as the target. The castle, the cobblestones, the cherry blossoms. All set to go kaput. But various delays meant that the B-29 bomber carrying the bomb didn't actually arrive in Kokura until just before midday. Which was just enough time for some grey clouds and smog to come in, in part due to the US firebombing a nearby city a few days before.

Under orders to aim for the munitions factory, the pilot made three full runs across the city to try to catch a glimpse of his target below. But 'at no time was the aiming point seen', he reported. 'I don't think our chances are very good.'

So he was ordered to fly to the fallback target. Nagasaki. A city that immediately became about 4000 degrees hotter. A city that immediately lost most of its buildings and about 70,000 of its people all because it was having a nice sunny day. (And a city, it's worth pointing out, that is still losing residents to this very day, thanks to unusually high rates of cancer.)

Kokura, on the other hand, is still as pristine as ever.

I think it's safe to say that Australians are doing well too when it comes to not being blown up. Since bombers were invented, back in about 1910, this country's soldiers have fought in something like twenty-nine wars – and our civilians have got through twenty-eight of them completely unscathed.

The one exception, of course, was WWII. Japan's bombing raids on Darwin on 19 February 1942, and then Broome two weeks later, are thought to have cost around 323 lives. Which is terrible. Awful. Please don't get me wrong. But it's worth remembering that these two raids were far from one-offs. Japanese bombers actually came to this country on no less than 109 other occasions .... for a total of no more than ten deaths. A number that is clearly ten more than ideal. But let's be honest, things could have been worse.

But here's the thing. Bombs aren't just dropped from above. They can also be hidden or thrown. Australians saw this first hand in the 1978 Sydney Hilton bombing, which killed three people, and at the 1986 Russell Street bombing, which killed a cop.

But these two tragedies aside, we've actually done pretty well in the small matter of staying alive.

Everyone was perfectly fine, for example, back in 1971, when an anonymous activist drove by the Soviet Embassy in Canberra at 3am and threw three homemade bombs over the fence. Going off right in the heart of the suburbs, and able to be heard over 8 kilometres away, the explosions shattered every window within 50 feet, destroyed the embassy's eaves and front door and gouged a massive hole in its driveway. Pieces of glass and stone flew in every direction, many of them travelling more than 150 feet.

But while fifty Russians had been asleep in the vicinity (and found themselves in need of new windows), all of them woke up without a scratch. Thanks, police said, to unusually thick curtains.

Yugoslavian diplomats also had to get in touch with a glazier after a bomb went off during a 1967 New Year's party in 1967, at the Consulate-General's office in Sydney's Double Bay. But it was a bomb that miraculously killed not a soul. Just like the two more that were detonated at the Yugoslav trade centre a few years later, right in the heart of the CBD. The first injured sixteen people. The second failed to go off. But once again, nobody died.

Both incidents were followed by an explosion five years after that, which destroyed another Yugoslav trade centre in Melbourne, damaging five shops and twenty houses nearby. 'It felt like an earth tremor,' said Laurie Fry, who lived a hundred metres away – and woke up to the sight of his baby daughter covered in broken glass. 'I dived out of bed. I thought a car had gone through our house. When I got outside, there were about sixty people crowded in the street. I could see there had been an explosion.' But the good news was, no one saw a dead body.

If you ever *did* have to see a dead body, I guess, Jack van Tongeren's may not be a bad choice. A sort of pseudo-Hitler, all the way down to the jackboots and small, black moustache, this Vietnam War veteran was in charge of the 'Australian Nationalist Movement' during the 1980s. Said 'movement' being a pathetically small group of Neo-Nazis who liked to parade around Perth wearing tight black pants over their tiny white willies.

In 1985, an ASIO agent showed why our spies get paid the big bucks, reporting this 'trained military killer ... has a pathological hatred of Asians, especially Vietnamese'. One of his clues seems to have been the thousands of 'Asians Out' posters that the ANM had been slapping on letterboxes, poles and bus stops all over Perth. The other seems to have been the thousands of other posters that read 'No Asians'.

But despite all the swastikas and sporadic street brawls, ASIO also seems to have decided that the 'threat posed to security is low' – and many Perth police officers appeared to agree with them. The jackbooted ones were 'a bit eccentric and full of wind, but basically quite sociable and friendly' reported one Constable O'Neill, while van

Tongeren himself later said that some police 'actually encouraged our plastering up teams in action, even the skinhead teams – and skinheads and police rarely get on well together. Many police vehicle patrols must have seen our teams in action but let us carry on.'

But that ~~blatant police racism~~ apparent police indifference all changed in September 1988 when the ANM decided to crank up its 'activism'. Over the following eight months, they firebombed no less than six Chinese restaurants – causing hundreds of thousands of dollars' worth of damage, but once again failing to injure a soul.

Or, rather, all that ~~blatant police racism~~ apparent police indifference *should* have changed in September 1988 – but according to the then-police minister, it didn't. 'On the question of taking action against people who were engaged in fire-bombings and wreaking havoc within the community, some police officers were loath to take action,' lamented Labor's Gordon Hill. 'Some of my colleagues had the attitude that if we just ignore it, it will go away.'

Luckily, however, the group needed to fund its activities, which meant that sooner or later they had to start robbing white people. Finally stung into action by the occurrence of actual crimes – crimes, that is to say, with actual, real, human victims – Perth's police force quickly swung into action. Within months, van Tongeran and co. were in prison.

And not a moment too soon. According to a summary of evidence from The *Canberra Times*, some of ANM's imminent plans for a better, purer, whiter Australia had included 'murdering senior police officers and a government minister, blowing up ships at Kwinana, south of Perth, nail-bombing a Vietnamese pool hall in Perth, breaking into the Maylands Police Academy and stealing weapons, and blowing out the walls of Fremantle Prison and arming the prisoners'.

But as the poet Robert Burns put it (somewhat confusingly), 'The best-laid schemes o' Mice an' Men/ Gang aft agley'. None of that stuff ever happened. Every now and then, crime does pay.

A life of crime did not, however, pay dividends for Hagop Levonian. A Sydney man of Armenian descent who was not such a fan of the Turks, he not the sort of person to keep his thoughts to himself. He was the sort to put a bomb in his car, and drive to Melbourne's Turkish consulate at 2am on a Saturday night, and park it right next door. The Turkish consulate was located just metres from Toorak Road, a bustling mecca of shops and cafes in the heart of Melbourne. The bomb was timed to go off on Monday morning, when said building would be full of people – just like all the shops, cafes and footpaths nearby.

Not a bad scheme, if you like that sort of thing, but it was also a scheme with a big, fatal flaw. Levonian didn't actually know how to set up the timer. Or perhaps he did but was just a bit of a duffer. All we know for sure is that his bomb went off then and there, at 2.16am, scattering his body in lots of small, bloody pieces.

Around twenty buildings were damaged in the blast, and more than a handful caught fire. But yet again, Australia's luck was in and no innocent people were hurt. Just as they weren't when protestors bombed a Queensland resort development back in 1980 and Perth's

French consulate in 1995. Levonian's family may not exactly concur, but on home soil, Australians have been very lucky.

Overseas, of course, the news is less positive. Terrorist attacks have claimed the lives of quite a few Aussie tourists – but on the plus side, Jimmy Barnes was just fine. The gravelly voiced Aussie rocker and his wife and baby grandson could easily have fallen victim to the huge bomb that destroyed a Bangkok shrine back in 2015, killing twenty-one people and injuring 123.

'We were literally staying at the Erawan Hotel, which is attached to the shrine,' Barnes told *A Current Affair*, 'and we had two ways of [leaving it]. We could literally go out the front door and turn right and walk past the shrine and across the road – which would have meant we would have been in the middle of the bomb blast.' But, exiting the hotel on that fateful morning, the couple spontaneously elected to turn left instead – because the crowds around the shrine were quite noisy and thick, and they were pushing a pram.

'We were literally 50 yards from the bomb,' Barnes recalled.

> The whole place shook, the windows were wobbling as if they were made out of plastic, it was a very frightening thing ... There was smoke, and sirens, and people running everywhere ... Had my grandson not been with us, had he not been in a pram and had it not been difficult, we would have walked straight into the bomb ... The little, tiny twists of fate and whatever it was, caring about the family or whatever, just made us make that decision and walk that way. We were incredibly lucky.

Even more incredible, perhaps, is the fact that this wasn't Barnesy's first bomb. The Working Class Man also happened to be in Kuta on 12 October 2002 – the day two suicide bombers blew up two bars, killing eighty-eight Australian tourists. He says that he and his wife had intended to be in the area when the bombs went off, but had been forced to go back to their room, because one of their young kids had been misbehaving.

Former AFL footballer, Dermott Brereton, tells a similar tale, albeit without the kid. Just seconds before the Sari nightclub exploded, he and his friends had been double-parked directly outside it, contemplating a quick drink before they drove to the airport.

> We used to always have one last drink at the Sari Club on the way home. There were six of us in the van ... [An American girl call Karri Casner] jumped out and walked into the Sari Club and we said, 'Come on, let's have our last drink.' But one of our mates said 'No, we're going to be late getting onto the plane' ... So we said, 'Oh, you bugger' [and stayed in the van]. Anyway, we drove about 400m down the road and the bags were piled up in the back of our [van], and we heard this almighty 'boom'. We literally ducked and went 'What the hell is that?' ... Some of us said, 'That sounds like an explosion! Pipes? Gas work? What do you reckon?'

Karri, sad to say, would have been able to tell them. Had she not already been dead.

Australia's Lucky Midway

How a wrong turn helped win WWII

'I would rather have a general who was lucky than one who was good.'

Napoleon Bonaparte

'How can I be happy?' is one of life's toughest questions (right behind 'Who watches *Sky News*?'). Some say that it's all about living in the moment; others that it's finding a purpose. Answers like 'family', 'friends', 'success' and 'self-esteem' all get tossed around a bit, while my partner seems to think that both our lives would be perfect if I could just learn how to vacuum.

Personally, I don't have much to say (other than that our carpet is fine). But I would add that, if you like a calm, peaceful life, not being invaded by Mongols is a good way to start. The most unstoppable military force in all history – and clearly among the most brutal – they murdered about 50 million people during the 13th century, and tortured, raped or enslaved tens of millions more. No land empire had ever been bigger or more drenched in tears, sweat and blood.

By 1274, Genghis Khan's grandson was in charge of 9 million square miles, stretching from Bulgaria all the way to Beijing. And so he thought, I clearly need a few more. That ruthless autocrat therefore dispatched a war fleet east to a group of little islands that now go by the name of Japan. And not just any fleet, mind you. We're talking around 800 huge warships filled with about 30,000 men: one of the largest fleets that the world had ever seen.

Japan's tiny handful of peasants and samurai did not stand a ghost of a chance.

But it was the Mongols that ended up being ghosts, instead, after a tropical cyclone literally pushed them back west. Dubbed 'the divine wind' – or, to use the local language, 'kamikaze' – it's said to have sunk at least a third of the Mongol fleet, killing more or less everybody aboard.

So in 1281, they tried again. This time, the Khan assembled an even bigger fleet: something in the region of 400 vessels, containing about 140,000 men. And, wouldn't you know it, the weather gods struck again. Yet another kamikaze came along at just the right moment to save Japan from another mass murder. More than half of the Mongol ships ended up at the bottom of the ocean in what's still called 'one of the largest and most disastrous attempts at a naval invasion in history'.

Thanks to two lucky cyclones, the plucky island was saved – and its border remained safe for the next 600 years.

By the 20th century, the winds had changed. Massive industrialism and successful wars with Russia, China and Korea had turned that once-defenceless little island into Asia's biggest superpower – and far and away its most militaristic. It was now Japan's smaller neighbours that had to worry about invasion. Smaller neighbours much like Australia.

A little after dawn on 9 December 1941, however, that worry became something like panic. Because it was on that date, of course, that Japanese fighter planes launched a surprise attack on Pearl Harbor, the Hawaiian home of the US Pacific Fleet. Designed to cripple the American war machine before it was even turned on, the bombing raid killed 2400 people, sank dozens of warships and destroyed port facilities and planes. Australia declared war later that day, in lockstep with the US and Great Britain.

Historians have since argued that the US got lucky in a way, insofar as the damage would have been much, much worse if Japan had sought to take out its fuel depots. Our ally was also fortunate that many of its sunken ships happened to be docked in shallow waters on the day, which meant that they could fairly easily be retrieved and repaired. And luckier still was the fact that the pride of the fleet – its three big aircraft carriers – all happened to not be there on the day.

In short, things could have been worse. But it goes without saying that they could have been better. For the time being, at least, the Japanese were the masters of the Pacific. Australia's allies were in no position to stop them from sailing south and conquering pretty much all they saw.

So head south they did, sweeping though Thailand, crushing Malaya and capturing Hong Kong, Burma and Singapore. Most of what's now Indonesia soon fell too, along with the Solomon Islands, and US bases in Guam and Wake Island. By May 1942, only the southern half of New Guinea stood between Australia and Hitler's newest, fiercest ally – an ally that had not lost a war in more than four centuries. And an ally that promptly began to bomb Darwin and Broome and send submarines right into Sydney Harbour.

With what few soldiers we had mostly elsewhere, fighting Hitler, Australia was essentially open for conquest. Even our prime minister at the time saw no point pretending otherwise, openly admitting that 'it is beyond our capacity to meet an attack of the weight the Japanese could launch'.

'It was a disaster,' says Dr Tom Lewis, who heads up the Darwin Military Museum. 'Australians had been fighting in Europe and the Far East, but now the war had come to us ... raising fears [of invasion] to a fever pitch.'

But with those three US aircraft carriers still afloat in the Pacific, and many of its sunken battleships being quickly rebuilt, Japan needed to find a way to end the war quickly. The US Navy was battered and bruised but getting get back on its feet. A big knockout blow was required.

To that end, Admiral Yamamoto began developing plans to seize a small US air base on a coral atoll, roughly midway between the United

States and Asia. Known as Midway Atoll, it was close (but not too close) to Hawaii – making it the perfect point from which to stage a big battle. On 4 June 1942 Japan's four major aircraft carriers wended their way towards American waters, accompanied by hundreds of planes, subs and ships. It was, in the words of US Intelligence officer Captain Edwin T Layton, an 'elite' and 'overwhelming force'. A force that had hitherto 'been the terror of the Pacific' and a nonstop source of 'destruction and fear'.

And that destruction and fear looked set to continue when Japanese bombers struck the US base a little bit before dawn. Sent out from the four aircraft carriers an hour to the west, and swooping and diving with deadly precision, the bombers destroyed oil depots, docks, hangars and buildings en masse, before flying back west to refuel and reload.

It was at least another hour before the United States was able to send out planes in response – but they didn't just come from the smouldering ruins of its base. Unbeknown to the Japanese, they had been making preparations for just such a raid and had three aircraft carriers of their own about an hour to the east.

But that did not necessarily mean that said planes knew where to go. Already separated from each other by dozens of miles, the US carriers each took more than ninety minutes to dispatch their hundreds of planes on the two-hour flight to a counterattack. That meant two hours of total radio silence, so the (equally scattered) Japanese fleet could not hear them coming. But it also meant two hours in which

Japanese aircraft carriers could continue to move around willy nilly, which meant that none of the US planes precisely knew where they'd be.

The result was an uncoordinated series of piecemeal attacks: different raids carried out on different ships by different squadrons at different times. The only consistent thing about the counteroffensive was its complete and total lack of success. By 9.30am, the Japanese fleet had seen off, or shot down, close to a dozen separate squadrons and in return, barely suffered a scratch.

Every single US plane had been either shot down or forced to fly back because they were about to run out of fuel. Every single plane, that is, except for a little squadron of thirty-two dive-bombers under the command of Lieutenant Wade McClusky. A squadron that had never even turned up to fight in the first place, because it had managed to get lost on the way.

By this time, the Japanese had naturally started to wonder where on earth all of these planes were coming from (the airbase at Midway Atoll not actually being that big). Did the United States have some aircraft carriers of its own floating somewhere nearby?

A spy plane radioed through the answer a little after 10am – just about the time that the Japanese had finished brushing off all those pesky US planes, and had almost finished rearming and refuelling their own planes for bombing raid number two.

The spy plane reported that, yes, their suspicions were correct: almost the entire US fleet was just two hours east. As far as the Japanese were concerned, this was excellent news. The big knockout fight that they needed was close at hand. And it was a fight they were sure they would win.

Overseeing operations from aboard the *Akagi*, Admiral Nagumo accordingly made ready for a major sea battle – which meant issuing three major orders. The first was that his fleet, which was scattered over hundreds of miles, quickly regroup by his side. The second was that the planes just back from Midway be fitted with torpedos (as they now needed to take on fast-moving boats). This meant removing the drop-bombs that the carrier staff had been busy installing for raid number two. Order three was to give the planes even more fuel, so they could stay up in the air for the length of the battle.

By 10.19am, therefore, all four Japanese aircraft carriers were bunched together and very much abuzz with activity. Piles of abandoned bombs lay here, there and everywhere, in between open fuel lines and torpedo-filled planes. If you think that sounds dicey, your thinking is sound. They were basically 'floating powder kegs'.

They were also basically ready to rumble, as Commander Mitsuo Fuchida later wrote:

> One after another, our planes were hoisted from the hangar and quickly arranged on the flight deck. There was no time to lose. At 10.20, Admiral Nagumo gave the order to launch when ready. On *Akagi*'s flight deck all planes were in position with engines warming up. The big ship began turning into the wind. Within five minutes all her planes would be launched.

Within five minutes, Australia's fate would be sealed.

And it was right at that moment that McClusky arrived.

Banned from using their radio, and by now desperately low on fuel, his squadron had been hopelessly lost for over three hours – flying in lonely circles through thick mist and fog many hundreds of miles to the north. But literally within seconds of being forced to turn back, they had managed to spot a small Japanese ship, travelling at super-high speed, through a tiny break in the clouds. The smart thing to do would have been to bomb it to hell, then turn back to refuel and reload. But some hunch made McClusky decide to follow it instead, on the off-chance that it would lead to something worth bombing.

It did. Obeying Admiral Nagumo's order to regroup for battle, the little ship led the bombers to all four Japanese aircraft carriers ... at precisely 10.20. At the precise moment in time when they had their pants down.

'The devastation was immediate and appalling.' In what historian John Keegan called 'the most stunning and decisive blow in the history of naval warfare', McClusky's little squadron sank three of Japan's four aircraft carriers in less than five minutes.

At 10.20, Japan was still winning the war, just as had been for the previous six months.

At 10.25, the war was effectively lost. The tide had turned. 'As a result of the US victory in the Battle of Midway, Japan abandoned its plan to expand its reach in the Pacific and would remain on the defensive for the remainder of World War II.'

It would take three more years for Japan to surrender. But it was right then and there, in the space of five lucky minutes, that the lucky country became a safe one again.

Lucky Breaks

Convicts who got out of jail

'Nobody gets justice. People only get good luck or bad luck.'

Orson Welles, American actor

Living in Australia can be punishing at times. The flights are long. The traffic is intense. Richard Wilkins still has a job. And if you want to buy a house without turning to crime you're probably looking at a lifetime of debt.

But when it comes to *actual* punishments, things probably aren't all that bad. Hanging, after all, was abolished way back in the 70s, flogging a little bit before that. I'm not saying that Australian jails would be a *pleasant* place to be. But if you're ever going to be caught committing a crime, I'd probably suggest you do it here rather than in, say, Iran.

Once upon a time, however, my advice would have been different. More than 165,000 convicts were transported from Britain to Australia between 1787 and 1868, and I think it's fair to say that they didn't have a great time. As Robert Hughes phrased it in *The Fatal Shore*, after months of lying 'on soaked bedding ... crusted with salt, shit and vomit', 'chilled to the bone' and 'festering with scurvy and boils', the prisoners arrived in a place that was 'more punitive in its conventions [and] more capricious in its workings' than the England they had left far behind.

Scattered up and down the east coast, Australia's penal camps were essentially 'a lottery ... whose losers were no better off than slaves'. Basic human rights were not really a thing. Standard punishments included hard labour and leg irons, floggings and hangings, starvation and solitary confinement. Murder and rape were far from uncommon; fleas, rats and disease absolutely routine.

'Flogging in this country is such a common thing that nobody thinks anything about it,' wrote one early visitor to the colony. Walking down a street in Bathurst one day, he 'saw a man walk across the yard with the blood that ran from his lacerated flesh squashing out his shoes at every step he took. A dog was licking the blood off the triangles, and the ants were carrying away great pieces of human flesh that the lash had scattered about the ground.'

Later taking it upon himself to see a flogging firsthand, he reported that the flogger's ...

> ... foot had worn a deep hole in the ground by the violence with which he whirled himself around on it to strike the quivering and wealed [sic]

back, out of which stuck the sinews, white, ragged and swollen. The infliction was a hundred lashes, at about half-minute time, so as to extend the punishment through nearly an hour.

In short, Australian prisons were painful beyond all imagining – and I say that as a parent who has been to primary school musicals. So it's pretty obvious why so many convicts tried their best to escape (just as I managed to do during *Bugsy Malone*). The only problem was that, surrounded as they were by oceans, desert and bush, escaping from an Australian prison was a great way to get lost.

And even if, by some freak chance, you happened to know where you were going, what you basically knew was that there was nowhere to go. To get away from a prison without getting shot was essentially to risk starvation, heatstroke, snakebite or a spear until the time came to get caught and hanged.

Still, at least some convicts managed to get away for good. Convicts like Miss Mary Bryant. Sentenced to hang for the grievous crime of stealing a lady's silk bonnet, this twenty-one-year-old had the good luck to receive a last-minute reprieve. And the bad luck to be sent to Australia aboard the boil-riddled First Fleet.

It didn't take long for this native of Cornwall to realise that Sydney was no place for her and so hatch a plan to escape. Together with her new husband, William (a convicted smuggler) and two even newer children (both aged under three), Mary and seven other convicts didn't just manage to steal a small open fishing boat. They somehow managed to sail all the way to Timor. That's over 5000 kilometres of choppy, mostly uncharted waters: sixty-nine days and sixty-nine nights of wind and waves, rain and reefs, next to no food and two whiney toddlers. That seems to me like a *Cats*-level nightmare. Maybe even a *Les Misérables*.

But somehow the eleven made it to the little Dutch colony ... only to be clapped in chains and sent back to England, to be tried for their shameful escape. And they may not have sailed in the most five-star of conditions, if anything can be read into the fact that four of them died from disease on the way. And another two threw themselves overboard.

Now a childless widow, Bryant arrived back in London in 1792 and was taken straight to Newgate Prison. Her next stop was clearly going to be the noose, given that the punishment for escape was death. Her luck, such as it was, seemed to have finally run out.

But in fact, it was only just getting started. With the London press in raptures about her unlikely escape, Bryant's story attracted the notice of a certain James Boswell. A wealthy and influential lawyer best known for his adoring biography of Dr Samuel Johnson, he was also a man who adored the chicks and never stopped trying to shag them. Along with nineteen separate STIs (syphilis and gonorrhoea being among the most painful), his diary mentions three full-time girlfriends, seven long-term mistresses and 'lusty embraces' with sixty sex workers. And that just covers a small slice of his twenties.

In short, we're talking about a man with a 'great curiosity to lubricate' more or less anyone, be they 'a monstrous big Whore' or a 'gross' 'wretch'. All a woman needed for Boswell to paw her was a pulse and four limbs. And he was probably prepared to compromise on the limbs.

Which brings us to Bryant, the young, winsome widow. While history doesn't record whether the two had an affair, we *do* know that Boswell was quick to visit her in prison after seeing her face in the papers – and then used his money and influence to secure her release. He also gave her £10 a year until his death some years later. As well as (one suspects) gonorrhoea.

But Mary wasn't the only convict to (possibly) sleep their way to freedom and in the process earn a measure of fame. Twenty-four years of age and hardly more than five foot, Ireland's John Graham managed to do much the same thing after being sent down under for stealing some hemp. Dispatched to what's now Brisbane – a penal settlement 'whose severity and cruelty ... constituted one of the greatest blots on the whole penal system' – he managed to slip away in 1827, while working on a chain gang out in the bush. The standard play at this point would have been for him to head south to Sydney, in search of a ship (and get lost, caught or killed on the way).

But for whatever reason, our hero decided to head north instead – trekking up the treacherous coast until he bumped into some locals somewhere near Noosa Heads. With the frontier wars heating up, and the Kabi Kabi people having a 'fierce reputation', it was around about this moment that he really should have been killed.

But as luck would have it, he was recognised instead, as the dead husband of a lady named Mamba. According to local historian Raymond J Warren, 'Her two sons, Murrowdooling and Caravanti, also agreed that this was indeed the returning spirit of their dead father and they readily accepted him as such.'

Confronted with a by-no-means easy choice between marriage and certain death, Graham seems to have pondered awhile, and then in due course chosen the former. Now known as Moilow, he spent the next six-and-a-half years living with the family.

But marriage can be hard, as we all know – and in a move that many spouses will understand, Graham seems to have eventually decided that he'd prefer life in prison. We don't exactly know what happened (and it may well be that Mamba had died), but we do know that in 1833 he returned to Brisbane to voluntarily resume a life of labour and chains.

And that life really ought to have continued, for years to come, were it not for stroke of luck number two. In 1836, a lady named Eliza Fraser had the ill fortune to be shipwrecked and stranded on an island that now bears her name, along with three other members of the ill-fated ship's crew. An island that Graham happened to be familiar with, from his six-and-a-half years in the region, and whose language and people he happened to know very well. Sent to Fraser Island to negotiate Eliza's 'rescue', he seems to have done so with ease. Probably because the locals did not actually want her there, and were just feeding and housing her to be nice.

Eliza, however, was not nice in return. In fact, she was not nice, full stop. Described by one of her three fellow 'captives' as 'a vixen and a terrible liar and the most artful and profane woman that ever lived', she spent the rest of her life contradicting their assertions they had in fact been extremely well cared-for. Later found guilty of lying to the courts while seeking compensation for 'a fate worse than death', she wrote at length about Fraser Island's 'cruel savages' and 'cannibals' (as well as its many spiteful women who were jealous of her 'pure beauty'). This was all terrible news for local race relations, but it was great news for Graham, all in all, insofar as he suddenly found himself a well-known hero. And, more to the point, pardoned and free.

Whether or not James Porter was a pure beauty, records tell us that he had a 'sharp wit'. The 'young cockney' was not, however, especially sharp when it came to burglary, so was 'convicted of stealing a quantity of silk and beaver' in 1821. Sent to Tasmania later that year, he made at least four separate attempts to escape the island – but was hunted down every time. 'I was fully determined,' he later wrote, 'to gain my point or perish in the attempt.'

Porter's main problem, clearly, was the lack of a ship. So in 1834, he tried a new tack – somehow managing to hijack a brand-new, yet-to-be-finished, 120-tonne brig called the *Frederick*, which had a £1200 fortune aboard. Miraculously, he then managed to sail it all the way to Chile, in the company of nine other convicts.

As Dan Franklin writes, it was 'a remarkable feat of navigation and sailing skill, made possible by a huge amount of luck'.

Sailing the [massive] *Frederick*, which was designed for hugging coastlines, not tackling the open ocean, was a tall order for 10 hands, five of whom had no experience. Its green planks sprung a leak and the only working bilge pump had to be manned round the clock. To make matters worse, they ran into several fierce gales.

The gales were so fierce, in fact, that the 'leaky and battered beyond repair' brig eventually began to sink, forcing the ten convicts to take a rowboat to shore.

The smart move, at that point, would have been to keep going. But Porter and three others instead chose to stay put in Chile, trusting the Spanish authorities to not give them up, given that they and the Brits were at war. This theory proved sound, for a couple of years. Until the day came that it didn't.

Taken back to Hobart in chains, the '*Frederick* Four' were charged with piracy – a serious crime that carried a sentence of death. But also, it turned out, a serious crime that local legislation decreed must take place upon 'the high seas'. As luck would have it, the brand-new brig had been docked in Macquarie Harbour at the time of being taken. And for that matter, it was yet to be registered, so was technically not even a ship.

Cleared on the most technical of technicalities, Porter avoided the hangman and returned to prison. And eventually managed to escape it for good.

The Jaws of Life

Aussies who survived being attacked by an animal

'With luck on your side, you can do without brains.'

Giordano Bruno, Italian philosopher

One of the great things about going overseas is that you get to meet brand-new people. People for whom your personality and lifestyle are a complete and total mystery. People who don't know you play Lego and still live with your mum. People who are prepared to have sex with you, or at the very least believe you are cool.

And, best of all, people with all sorts of strange preconceptions about what being an Australian actually tends to involve. The chief one, of course, is that it involves being super-outdoorsy. In real life, of course, Australians are some of the most urban people on the planet, and among the most lazy and overweight. We are a nation of suburbs and towns. A nation of couches and air conditioners and Netflix and TikTok. A nation where people will happily sit in traffic eating chips for an hour if the only alternative is to walk thirty minutes.

But tell a foreigner that you are from the land down under, and you may as well be Bear Grylls. To them, you are rugged and outdoorsy – a tough, hardy, adventurous type who spends all their time looking ripped on a surfboard, camping in the bush or doing something with sheep. Personally my bushcraft begins and ends with the ability to book a hotel. But when I'm overseas, it seems to go without saying that I know how to pitch a tent, light a fire and hunt down my dinner prey using nothing but a swag and some sticks.

And it goes without saying that I laugh in the face of danger – because danger is something that I face every day. To live in Australia is to live in a land full of animals that are trying to kill you. And a land where they often succeed.

On one level, I guess, this perception makes a certain kind of sense. Australia is indeed home to some spectacularly venomous animals, be they box jellyfish or blue-ringed octopuses, or our dozen or so deadly species of snakes. Throw in the spiders and stonefish and crocodiles and sharks and it's easy to see why people get me confused with Steve Irwin, even though I shriek at the sight of a mouse.

But at the same time, this perception makes no sense at all. Australia is a very large place, after all, and such creatures generally live far away. We pudgy urbanites don't have much to fear – and if you don't believe me, take a look at the maths.

Worldwide, according to CNET, animals kill something in the

region of 1.1 million people a year (mostly by way of insect-borne disease). This averages out to around 5500 people per country, per year.

In Australia, on the other hand, it's around thirty-two per year. No Australian has actually died from a spider bite since the late 1920s. And while snakebites kill about 100,000 people a year throughout the world, in the land down under, the figure is closer to two. Statistically speaking, you're a lot more likely to be killed while climbing a ladder, or taking a fall from your couch, bed or chair.

And even if you do happen to be one of the thirty-two Australians killed by an animal this year, there's every chance that it won't be a 'bad' one. Of the Aussies who met that fate between 2001 and 2017, well over half either fell from a horse, or swerved their car to avoid a dog, cat or cow. Even the sweet little honeybee kills more of us every year than, say, a croc or a shark.

Still, I would not necessarily suggest making friends with an eastern brown snake – though better one of them than, say, Andrew Bolt. Every bit as venomous as that *Herald Sun* columnist, though obviously not quite as unlikeable, they have been known to leap out and bite people for no apparent reason. And you really don't want to be there when they do.

Practically painless, so small and fine are its fangs, a brown snake's bite might not seem like a big deal at first. Sure, you might faint for a bit. Or get a touch weak and dizzy. Or sweat a lot or have a few major spews. But after the first fifteen minutes, you will often feel fine. Right up until the time you start bleeding to death.

'The venom makes you clot, tiny little clots over and over again, thousands of times,' according to Naren Gunja, a toxicologist with the University of Sydney.

This causes the body to use up all its clotting ability, called clotting factors. You run out of these clotting factors within a few hours. Then you start bleeding; bleeding in the brain, bleeding in the abdomen, bleeding in the chest and from the bite site.

The good news, if you don't have access to antivenom, is that this bleeding will eventually stop. The bad news, if you don't have access to antivenom, is that this will be because you are dead.

Such a prognosis wasn't news to Petrine Poole when her two-year-old was bitten back in 2022. 'He just said "Mum, a snake bit my leg,"' she told Channel 7 News, after a horrifying ordeal that saw her and her husband speed to Mudgee hospital, some 80 kilometres from their home town of Bylong.

'Leaving the house, we were panicked, we didn't even know what direction to drive,' Petrine said. 'The drive was 40 minutes of sheer hell. Because we didn't know if it was 40 minutes of precious time being wasted, it was horrible. But he was so ridiculously brave.'

More bravery was required, however, when the paramedics found not one but two brown-snake bites on his leg. 'That's when I feared the absolute worst,' Petrine said. 'I immediately thought, "Oh my God it's had a real go at him. How bad is it? How's he going to survive it?"'

How? How? I'll tell you how. By virtue of the strange and remarkable fact that neither of these brown-snake bites actually contained any venom. Brown snakes will very occasionally just bite for the purpose of self-defence – though for one to do so twice is nothing less than extraordinary. 'I'd say the young fellow's just had a little defensive bite. And he's gotten away really, really lucky,' said Billy Collett from the Australian Reptile Park.

Perhaps just as lucky, from the not-dying-a-horrible-death point of view, was a Perth businessman named Bernie Williams. A keen diver in his spare time, he was off the WA coast back in 2006 with a couple of equally keen diver friends. Floating about a craggy reef, the forty-six-year-old managed to find some crayfish and a couple of shells, but in the process lose both of his friends. Which was fine, in a sense, because he was about to make a brand-new one.

Though in another sense, this was no friend at all.

'It came up from below, behind, and rammed me, just hammered me,' Bernie said of the massive great white shark that suddenly came out of nowhere and crashed right into his back. 'I am not very small and for something to take me from zero to 100 kilometres an hour in a fraction of a second, bending me double, you think, "God, have I been hit by a submarine?" It was just so solid. It felt like a brick wall.'

Unfortunately, though, this was a brick wall with teeth: big, sharp teeth that clamped themselves around his arm and dragged him at speed through the water. 'I was stunned, didn't know what was going on [but] when it slowed down a bit I could swing my head around. A shark's eyeball literally filled my face mask [and] it was swinging me around like a dog with a goanna.'

Happily, Williams' friends had thought to bring shark shields (a sort of anklet that emits an electromagnetic field that sharks dislike and generally try to avoid). Less happily, he didn't have one. What he did have, however, was a spear gun holstered on his left hip – a long, sharp piece of metal that clearly irked his new friend to the point where it briefly let him go ... just above a conveniently shaped ledge in the reef.

> I was hunched down but there wasn't enough room for me to get everything in there. I was really puffing hard, breathing like a steam train, beginning to hyperventilate ... I remember hearing my heart banging. Banging away, banging away, thinking to myself, 'I'm dead, I'm dead, I'm dead. This thing has got my name punched ... It's not going away.' ... Next thing, it came flying across the reef at me ... It was like a dart. The distance would have been 15 to 20 metres and it covered that in a couple of seconds.

While the diver 'had just enough time to lift my spear gun and ... fend it off', the shark took a second bite in the process. 'The girth of the thing. Like a car going over. Massive. Absolutely massive.' With 'blood making the water shimmery' and a 'woozy' Williams 'beginning to fade', the shark circled back and began to charge once again. And it continued to charge to 'within a couple of metres [when] all of a sudden it did a shimmy in the water, turned its tail and took off'.

Williams' friends – and, more to the point, their shark shields – had happened to swim by just in time.

Equally fortunate when it came to his friends was a Cape York mine worker named Todd Bairstow. An avid pig hunter and fisherman (ladies, please form a queue), that twenty-eight-year-old got a taste of what it was like to be hunted himself while fishing alone back in 2001. Alone on the banks of a river in Weipa, he was quietly reeling in a line when a 3.2 metre crocodile leapt out the water, latched on to his legs and attempted to drag him in. I say 'attempted', because Bairstow somehow managed to grab onto a mangrove branch and cling on for dear life.

Thirty minutes, three 'death rolls' and two broken legs later, Bairstow was still clinging on. But, by this stage knee-deep in water, he later said that he 'was just about to let go. I couldn't do it anymore. It felt like my arms were just going to snap off. I was thinking: right, do I drown myself or get eaten alive?'

Fortunately, the answer was neither. A woman heard him screaming from a pub 350 metres away, and within minutes his mate, Kevin Beven, was on the bank, pulling him from the beast's jaws.

'And then these four Aboriginal fellas arrived, hitting the croc with rocks and sticks until it pissed off back into the water,' Mr Bairstow said.

Not a bad story, all in all. As a matter of fact, I might even pinch it for myself when I'm next overseas.

Conclusion

I believe the children are our future. Which is quite frankly a cause for concern. I don't wish to sound like I'm being critical in any way, but we're talking about people with the attention span of a newt and the work ethic of a newt who is sleeping. A generation of people who use 'snack' as an adjective and 'steez' as a noun, people who deliberately say shit like 'cheugy' and 'simp'.

It's not that Gen Z are without their good qualities. (They must have some somewhere, I'm sure.) But is a lifetime spent on TikTok while wearing shit clothes really the best preparation for the big world outside? A world that looks certain to be filled with droughts and famine and flood and wars and even more albums by Justin Bieber?

IDK, as they say. But I do know this. If they're living in Australia, they're certain to have lots of luck on the way.

And I joke. We are lucky to have them.

Acknowledgements

The author would like to thank Ruby, Keiran and all the other fine people at Affirm Press for being fine people and also good publishers.

Also by Eamon Evans

Who stole the priceless Picasso from the NGV? Was Errol Flynn a Nazi spy? Did an Australian kill the infamous Red Baron?

If you think Australia's history is straightforward, you're dead wrong. This is a land of the strange, the spooky and the unexplained. From the eerie ball of light that stalked a terrified family across the Nullarbor, to the whereabouts of Victoria's parliamentary mace, to the unidentified body found propped up on an Adelaide beach, and, yes, to the whereabouts of Ned Kelly's skull, you'll find our history has plenty of mysterious twists and unanswered questions.

With his signature wit, Eamon Evans investigates Australia's most curious mysteries, digs up the evidence and lays it out for the court of public opinion to decide. *Whatever Happened to Ned Kelly's Head?* will have you scratching your head and wondering long after the last page.

Also by Eamon Evans

Vikings were on mushrooms. Booze may have cost us Gallipoli. The Nazis loved meth, and the Stone Age was more like the 'stoned age'.

We tend to see the past as a dull, sober place – as a time of stiff collars and straight-laced conformity, when people's bodies were as pure as their minds. We need to think again.

It turns out that many of the great events in history wouldn't have happened if someone hadn't got smashed. From presidents and prime ministers, soldiers and scientists, to explorers, writers, musos and more, many of mankind's great movers and shakers might have been better off having a quiet lie-down. And there's no one better placed to shine a light on their secrets than the ever-witty – and occasionally coherent – Eamon Evans.

Substance by substance and binge by binge, *Tanked* is your guide to all the trashy little moments that have helped change the course of our world.

Also by Eamon Evans

Satanists in Perth. Panthers in Sydney. Inner Melbourne's secret morgue.

Australia is stuffed full of stories that need to be taken with a big spoon of salt. Stories that we all know are silly, but that we also just can't help sharing. In *Great Australian Urban Legends*, Eamon Evans presents you with myths, misconceptions and bare-faced lies about real people and real places down under. These pages libel Captain Cook and slander Phar Lap. They will annoy the Wiggles and David Boon. They will reveal whether Harold Holt really died, if the bunyip ever lived, and which famous Australian now gets by as a ghost.